| Human Migration

Other Books of Related Interest

Opposing Viewpoints Series

The Blockade of the Gaza Strip
The Politics of Water Scarcity
Sanctuary Cities

At Issue Series

Biological and Chemical Weapons
Environmental Racism and Classism
Migrant Workers

Current Controversies Series

Deporting Immigrants
Environmental Catastrophe
Globalization

| "Congress shall make
no law ... abridging
the freedom of speech,
or of the press."

First Amendment to the US Constitution

The basic foundation of our democracy is the First Amendment guarantee of freedom of expression. The Opposing Viewpoints series is dedicated to the concept of this basic freedom and the idea that it is more important to practice it than to enshrine it.

OPPOSING
VIEWPOINTS®
SERIES

Human Migration

Barbara Krasner, Book Editor

GREENHAVEN
PUBLISHING

Published in 2020 by Greenhaven Publishing, LLC
353 3rd Avenue, Suite 255, New York, NY 10010

Articles in Greenhaven Publishing anthologies are often edited for length to meet page
requirements. In addition, original titles of these works are changed to clearly present
the main thesis and to explicitly indicate the author's opinion. Every effort is made to
ensure that Greenhaven Publishing accurately reflects the original intent of the authors.
Every effort has been made to trace the owners of the copyrighted material.

Cover image: Ajdin Kamber/Shutterstock.com

Library of Congress Cataloging-in-Publication Data

Names: Krasner, Barbara, editor.
Title: Human migration / Barbara Krasner, book editor.
Description: First edition. | New York : Greenhaven Publishing, 2020. | Series: Opposing
viewpoints | Includes bibliographical references and index. | Audience: Grades 9–12.
Identifiers: LCCN 2019022826 | ISBN 9781534505995 (library
binding) | ISBN 9781534505988 (paperback)
Subjects: LCSH: United States—Emigration and immigration—Government policy—
Juvenile literature. | Immigrants—Government policy—United States—Juvenile
literature. | Refugees—Government policy—United States—Juvenile literature.
Classification: LCC JV6483 .H86 2020 | DDC 325.73—dc23
LC record available at https://lccn.loc.gov/2019022826

Manufactured in the United States of America

Website: http://greenhavenpublishing.com

Contents

Chapter 3: Do Immigrants Weaken a Country?

The Importance of Opposing Viewpoints

Perhaps every generation experiences a period in time in which the populace seems especially polarized, starkly divided on the important issues of the day and gravitating toward the far ends of the political spectrum and away from a consensus-facilitating middle ground. The world that today's students are growing up in and that they will soon enter into as active and engaged citizens is deeply fragmented in just this way. Issues relating to terrorism, immigration, women's rights, minority rights, race relations, health care, taxation, wealth and poverty, the environment, policing, military intervention, the proper role of government—in some ways, perennial issues that are freshly and uniquely urgent and vital with each new generation—are currently roiling the world.

If we are to foster a knowledgeable, responsible, active, and engaged citizenry among today's youth, we must provide them with the intellectual, interpretive, and critical-thinking tools and experience necessary to make sense of the world around them and of the all-important debates and arguments that inform it. After all, the outcome of these debates will in large measure determine the future course, prospects, and outcomes of the world and its peoples, particularly its youth. If they are to become successful members of society and productive and informed citizens, students need to learn how to evaluate the strengths and weaknesses of someone else's arguments, how to sift fact from opinion and fallacy, and how to test the relative merits and validity of their own opinions against the known facts and the best possible available information. The landmark series Opposing Viewpoints has been providing students with just such critical-thinking skills and exposure to the debates surrounding society's most urgent contemporary issues for many years, and it continues to serve this essential role with undiminished commitment, care, and rigor.

The key to the series's success in achieving its goal of sharpening students' critical-thinking and analytic skills resides in its title—

Opposing Viewpoints. In every intriguing, compelling, and engaging volume of this series, readers are presented with the widest possible spectrum of distinct viewpoints, expert opinions, and informed argumentation and commentary, supplied by some of today's leading academics, thinkers, analysts, politicians, policy makers, economists, activists, change agents, and advocates. Every opinion and argument anthologized here is presented objectively and accorded respect. There is no editorializing in any introductory text or in the arrangement and order of the pieces. No piece is included as a "straw man," an easy ideological target for cheap point-scoring. As wide and inclusive a range of viewpoints as possible is offered, with no privileging of one particular political ideology or cultural perspective over another. It is left to each individual reader to evaluate the relative merits of each argument—as he or she sees it, and with the use of ever-growing critical-thinking skills—and grapple with his or her own assumptions, beliefs, and perspectives to determine how convincing or successful any given argument is and how the reader's own stance on the issue may be modified or altered in response to it.

This process is facilitated and supported by volume, chapter, and selection introductions that provide readers with the essential context they need to begin engaging with the spotlighted issues, with the debates surrounding them, and with their own perhaps shifting or nascent opinions on them. In addition, guided reading and discussion questions encourage readers to determine the authors' point of view and purpose, interrogate and analyze the various arguments and their rhetoric and structure, evaluate the arguments' strengths and weaknesses, test their claims against available facts and evidence, judge the validity of the reasoning, and bring into clearer, sharper focus the reader's own beliefs and conclusions and how they may differ from or align with those in the collection or those of their classmates.

Research has shown that reading comprehension skills improve dramatically when students are provided with compelling, intriguing, and relevant "discussable" texts. The subject matter of these collections could not be more compelling, intriguing, or urgently relevant to today's students and the world they are poised to inherit. The anthologized articles and the reading and discussion questions that are included with them also provide the basis for stimulating, lively, and passionate classroom debates. Students who are compelled to anticipate objections to their own argument and identify the flaws in those of an opponent read more carefully, think more critically, and steep themselves in relevant context, facts, and information more thoroughly. In short, using discussable text of the kind provided by every single volume in the Opposing Viewpoints series encourages close reading, facilitates reading comprehension, fosters research, strengthens critical thinking, and greatly enlivens and energizes classroom discussion and participation. The entire learning process is deepened, extended, and strengthened.

For all of these reasons, Opposing Viewpoints continues to be exactly the right resource at exactly the right time—when we most need to provide readers with the critical-thinking tools and skills that will not only serve them well in school but also in their careers and their daily lives as decision-making family members, community members, and citizens. This series encourages respectful engagement with and analysis of opposing viewpoints and fosters a resulting increase in the strength and rigor of one's own opinions and stances. As such, it helps make readers "future ready," and that readiness will pay rich dividends for the readers themselves, for the citizenry, for our society, and for the world at large.

Introduction

> *"There is a wide difference between closing the door altogether and throwing it entirely open."*
> —Alexander Hamilton[1]

In the above quote from 1802, American founding father and immigrant Alexander Hamilton sums up the crux of heated debate surrounding immigration that is still taking place today, more than two centuries later, amid the influx of immigrants to America and European countries. There is a difference between immigrants entering these countries legally and illegally between official ports of entry. There is a difference for refugees escaping war and persecution. There is a difference for adult and child.

Republicans and Democrats have opposing viewpoints about immigration in America. President Trump and many of his followers on the right advocate for closed doors and the expiration of protection for refugees and children brought into the country illegally. Those who do not support the president argue for the continuation of protected status and the upholding of constitutional rights. Conflict has emerged between state and federal government over immigration issues.

President Trump has proposed building a physical wall between the United States and Mexico to protect the border from human and drug trafficking as well as terrorism. The construction of a wall could be costly, however. President Trump has proposed that Mexico pay for that wall. He has been accused of wanting to end the Deferred Action for Children Act (DACA) as a means of politically dashing the American Dream in favor of a wall. But others argue that no wall is needed at all. Increased military presence could protect the border. Still there are experts who believe too many immigrants enter the United States illegally and that puts a drain on American resources and jobs.

Sometimes, an immigrant migrating with or without his family cares only about safety. Reports indicate that even if he attempts to enter the United States in an official fashion, he can be turned away. Debates ensue about the viability of Temporary Protected Status for immigrant refugees. Some pundits contend that special rules should apply to refugees for humanitarian reasons. The US Citizenship and Immigration Services (USCIS) has stipulated certain eligibility requirements for those affected by natural disaster, war, and persecution. However, others believe that anyone entering the country illegally should be deported. Certain cities have been named sanctuary cities, and these have proclaimed they will support all immigrants. The Center for Immigration Studies lists thirty-seven such cities, including Los Angeles, San Francisco, Chicago, Philadelphia, and New York City. It also lists numerous counties and eight states that offer immigrant sanctuary.[2]

Opinions are mixed about the value immigrants offer to a country. Once an immigrant enters the country, does he or she contribute to the country or place a burden on its resources? According to a 2019 Pew Research study, immigrants around the world represent more strength than drain.[3]

Economic impact is just one issue, however. Increased crime rates have been associated with immigrants. Legal experts indicate that this is a myth, popularized even by President Trump. But crime rates may increase if immigrants settle in neighborhoods with multiple cultures.

The ability of immigrants to learn English, some experts say, can help them develop basic survival skills and position themselves to understand and ensure their rights. This raises the issue of whether English should be a requirement for all immigrants throughout the country. Questions of special treatment for immigrants, especially illegal immigrants arise, as some states grant them in-state tuition while others may have to pay higher rates. Employment, too, earns the ire of some government officials. They want to stop the process of hiring highly-skilled workers on H-1B employment visas, much to the dismay of corporate employers who seek the talent and skills of these workers.

Tolerance of a high rate of immigrants has been an American issue for more than a hundred years. The issue seems to speak to the very foundation of the country's origins. As President Obama said in a 2014 speech, "We are and always will be a nation of immigrants. We were strangers once, too."[4]

The diverse perspectives in *Opposing Viewpoints: Human Migration* explore the complex issues surrounding immigration. In chapters titled "How Should the United States Control Its Borders?" "Should Special Rules Apply to Refugee Immigrants?" "Do Immigrants Weaken a Country?" and "Should DACA and Dreamers Be Allowed to Continue?" viewpoint authors tackle challenging and compelling questions. These questions encompass legal, demographic, socio-economic, and ethical issues debated by politicians, policymakers, scholars, researchers, journalists, and other professionals.

Notes

1. Alexander Hamilton, "The Examination Number VIII [12 January 18020," National Archives Founders Online, accessed May 27, 2019, https://founders.archives.gov/documents/Hamilton/01-25-02-0282.
2. Bryan Griffith and Jessica M. Vaughan, "Maps: Sanctuary Cities, Counties, and States," April 16, 2019, accessed May 27, 2019, https://cis.org/Map-Sanctuary-Cities-Counties-and-States.
3. Ana Gonzalez-Barrera and Phillip Connor, "Around the World, More Say Immigrants Are a Strength Than a Burden," Pew Research Center, March 14, 2019, accessed May 27, 2019, https://www.pewglobal.org/2019/03/14/around-the-world-more-say-immigrants-are-a-strength-than-a-burden/.
4. Office of the Press Secretary, "Remarks by the President to the Nation on Immigration," White House President Barack Obama, November 20, 2014, accessed May 27, 2019, https://obamawhitehouse.archives.gov/the-press-office/2014/11/20/remarks-president-address-nation-immigration.

OPPOSING
VIEWPOINTS®
SERIES

CHAPTER 1

How Should the United States Control Its Borders?

Chapter Preface

With millions of unauthorized immigrants living in the United States, the federal government has been seeking ways to put "America First" and let Americans enjoy the benefits of living in this country. Some claim that there are simply too many undocumented workers who take jobs away from Americans. This is not a new way of thinking, since America has always been a nation where natives and strangers coexisted. President Trump has proposed legislation to build a wall to protect America's southern borders against illegal immigration, human trafficking, and drug trafficking. That proposal has met with heated debate.

Some experts believe putting up a wall to deter illegal immigration from the Mexican border is unnecessary. They maintain that technology could help identify those entering the country illegally. This approach could allow border patrol employees to more efficiently use their time to apprehend lawbreakers. Experts also observe that in the past twenty years increased funding in border control resources has not brought expected results. Economists put forth a view that asks policymakers to change the cost-benefit equation. From a worker's perspective, the sacrifices of crossing the border are worth the risk to earn about ten times as much money in a month in the United States.

But it's not just about economics. If an unauthorized immigrant and his family make it into the country, policies may force the separation of that family. The worker may face criminal legal proceedings and deportation. The children may become custody of the US government. Would a wall keep families together and force legal immigration? Or, should policies change, as some experts argue, to allow families to stay intact?

The following chapter investigates government policies and intended legislation to deter immigrant entrance into the United States. The viewpoints express different perspectives about the advantages and disadvantages of tightened border security.

> *"In the first six months of the current fiscal year, the U.S. border patrol apprehended 120,700 people from the Northern Triangle countries attempting to enter the U.S. Some of those who cross the border will apply for asylum, but the majority will be sent back to their countries of origin and the violence they were fleeing."*

Trump's Stance on Border Security Helped Put Him in the White House

Danielle Douez

In the following viewpoint, Danielle Douez presents immigration-related statements made by President Trump during the 2016 presidential campaign and compares them to the facts cited by experts. In campaign rallies and press interviews, then-candidate Trump made bold and somewhat shocking statements indicating that as president he would be tough on immigration, even tougher and much less merciful than his predecessor. His "Muslim ban" and proclamations that he would build the biggest and best wall to prohibit illegal immigration from Mexico and points south inflamed debate surrounding immigration, boosting his supporters and further alienating his detractors. Danielle Douez is associate editor of politics and society for the Conversation.

As you read, consider the following questions:

1. Do Trump's ideas about immigration match up with those of immigration experts, according to the viewpoint?
2. Do the experts cited in this viewpoint believe a bigger border wall is the solution?
3. Does that fact that Trump ran on these immigration policies indicate that Americans agree with him?

D onald Trump took a last-minute trip to Mexico on Wednesday. He met with President Enrique Peña Nieto before appearing at a rally in Arizona, in which he sought to clarify his positions on immigration.

Those who were hoping to hear him soften his tone in an attempt to expand his base were disappointed. Trump talked tough:

> "We will break the cycle of amnesty and illegal immigration. We will break the cycle. There will be no amnesty. Our message to the world will be this: You cannot obtain legal status or become a citizen of the United States by illegally entering our country."

But, do his ideas about immigration make sense in light of what experts say? Here are highlights of The Conversation's coverage of immigration issues.

The Wall, the Ban

If elected, Trump said he will build a wall between the U.S. and Mexico, and make Mexico pay for it. But a wall may not be necessary, according to migration data. David Cook Martín, a professor of sociology at Grinnell College, writes that thousands of Mexicans are leaving the U.S. of their own accord and returning to Mexico for a variety of reasons.

> "The study shows a net loss of 140,000 Mexican immigrants from the United States. One million Mexican migrants and their children left the U.S. for Mexico, while just over 860,000 left Mexico for the United States."

Of course, Mexicans are certainly not the only people crossing the U.S. border. Caitlin Fouratt, a professor of international studies at California State University, Long Beach writes about the thousands of Central Americans fleeing violence in Guatemala, Honduras and El Salvador—a region known as the Northern Triangle.

> "In the first six months of the current fiscal year, the U.S. border patrol apprehended 120,700 people from the Northern Triangle countries attempting to enter the U.S. Some of those who cross the border will apply for asylum, but the majority will be sent back to their countries of origin and the violence they were fleeing."

Trump has also previously called for a ban on Muslim immigrants. Scholars deemed this position un-American, as Sahar Aziz, professor of law at Texas A&M University writes:

> "At a time when most Americans are taught that our nation is post-racial and that we have moved beyond Japanese internment or Chinese exclusion laws, Trump's statements and consequent rise in the polls remind us that our nation has not advanced as much as we'd like to believe."

The 11 Million Here

Another major focus of U.S. immigration debate has been finding a solution for the estimated 11 million immigrants who already live in the U.S. without a visa or a pathway to citizenship.

Trump criticized President Obama's use of executive action to create a program to shield immigrants brought to the U.S. as children from deportation. Obama also created a similar program for parents of children who are U.S. citizens in 2014—Deferred Action for Parents of Americans.

In U.S. vs. Texas, 26 states refused to enforce the program and challenged Obama's use of executive action. The case went to the Supreme Court, and in June, the Court reached a 4-4 deadlock decision. Shana Tabak, professor of law at Georgia State University writes:

"Now, the millions who would have been eligible remain stranded, fearful of deportation and unable to legally work... This executive action represented an opportunity for many to finally come out of the shadows. President Obama's previous executive action, DACA, has dramatically improved the lives of many who were brought to the U.S. as children, allowing them to attend college, work, hold driver's licenses—to contribute to the societies of which they are a part."

Trump's plan also highlighted enforcing deportation of undocumented immigrants by tripling the number of Immigration and Customs Enforcement agents and creating a special deportation taskforce. What would be the effect of such a policy?

Miliann Kang, professor of Women, Gender and Sexuality Studies at the University of Massachusetts Amherst points out that mass deportation has and would have continued negative effects on millions of children who are born in the U.S. and are legal U.S. citizens.

"Sammy is a teenager I recently met who was born and raised in the Southwest. His parents were living in the U.S., working and raising their children, until they were stopped for a traffic violation, or audited for taxes, or turned in by a teacher or medical provider, or any of the mundane ways that undocumented status gets uncovered. Now Sammy is living with foster parents."

> *"Please go back, you will not be admitted into the United States unless you go through the legal process. This is an invasion of our Country and our Military is waiting for you!"*

Will Increasing Border Troops Stop Illegal Immigration?

David Smith and David Agren

In the following viewpoint David Smith and David Agren analyze the strategy behind President Trump's decision to send a disproportionate number of US military troops to the southern border. The move was ostensibly a reaction to migrant caravans making their way north from Central America. However, the authors quote several experts who note that the deployment occurred right before midterm elections, the implication being that Trump was stoking fear and acting upon it only in the interest of votes. David Smith is Washington bureau chief for the Guardian. *David Agren covers Mexico for* the Guardian *and other publications.*

"Trump announces plan for US military to guard Mexican border 'until we can have a wall,'" by David Smith, Guardian News and Media Limited, April 3, 2018. Reprinted by permission.

As you read, consider the following questions:

1. How many US troops were deployed to the Mexican border compared to the number stationed in Syria?
2. What does the author claim Trump's motives were in deploying the troops?
3. According to the article, have illegal border crossings increased or declined?

D onald Trump is to deploy more than 5,200 troops to the border with Mexico in what a rights organisation described as an abuse of the military to "further his anti-immigrant agenda of fear and division".

The announcement, just days before the midterm elections, came as Mexico also cracked down on migrants attempting to cross its own porous southern border.

General Terrence O'Shaughnessy, the head of US northern command, said 800 US troops were already en route to the Texas border and 5,200 would be headed to the south-west region by the end of the week, far higher than the 800 to 1,000 initially forecast.

There are about 2,000 US troops deployed in Syria to combat Islamic State, according to the Pentagon.

"That is just the start of this operation," O'Shaughnessy told reporters. "We will continue to adjust the number and inform you of those. But please know that is in addition to the 2,092 that are already employed from our national guard troops."

The troops will provide "mission-enhancing capabilities" at ports of entry in Texas, Arizona and California, officials added, and will be armed. They will also have use of helicopters with night-vision capabilities and sensors.

A caravan of several thousand Central American migrants—including entire families and elderly people—has been moving slowly north since mid-October and is now in southern Mexico. They are still 2,000 miles by road and weeks away from reaching a US port of entry, where most are expected to seek asylum as the law allows.

But Trump, who stoked anger and fear over illegal immigration on his way to winning the 2016 presidential election, has seized on the caravan at campaign rallies ahead of next week's midterm polls, hoping the issue will again fire up his core support.

On Monday he warned that the military would be waiting. "Many Gang Members and some very bad people are mixed into the Caravan heading to our Southern Border," Trump tweeted. "Please go back, you will not be admitted into the United States unless you go through the legal process. This is an invasion of our Country and our Military is waiting for you!" he added.

The American Civil Liberties Union condemned the latest move as political opportunism.

Shaw Drake, policy counsel at its rights centre in El Paso, Texas, said: "President Trump has chosen just before midterm elections to force the military into furthering his anti-immigrant agenda of fear and division. But this harmful action is nothing more than Trump's latest aggression against immigrant families with children who seek our protection. These migrants need water, diapers and basic necessities—not an army division."

Drake added: "Sending active military forces to our southern border is not only a huge waste of taxpayer money, but an unnecessary course of action that will further terrorize and militarize our border communities. Military personnel are legally prohibited from engaging in immigration enforcement, and there is no emergency or cost-benefit analysis to justify this sudden deployment."

Mexico, meanwhile, has also been tightening security on its southern border, where migrants often use rafts to cross the Suchiate river.

On Monday, Mexican marines patrolled the river as people tried to swim and wade across.

Video shared with the Guardian shows a marine in a patrol boat yelling into a megaphone: "This is to save human lives and provide humanitarian assistance. The river conditions are not optimal for being able to cross swimming."

Another video posted on social media shows a government helicopter hovering low over the water, creating turbulent conditions for the immigrants trying to cross the river.

On Sunday, one migrant died after he was hit with a rubber bullet when Mexican federal police rebuffed another group of migrants who tried to enter the country over the international bridge.

Mexico's interior minister, Alfonso Navarrete, said on Sunday night the police were not equipped with any such weapon and had come under attack as immigrants threw rocks, bottles and firecrackers. Guatemala's interior ministry claimed the group trying to cross the border had wounded Guatemalan police and used children as human shields.

Mexico routinely complains about the treatment of its own citizens living in the US without the proper papers, but has been detaining and deporting Central Americans in large numbers since 2014.

Statistics from US Customs and Border Protection (CBP) show that illegal border crossings have declined significantly from record highs in the early years of the century.

Last year, 396,579 undocumented people were apprehended after entering the US illegally. In 2000, more than 1.6 million illegal border crossers were apprehended.

> "Its border enforcement strategies are failing on their own terms and, until the United States reassesses its overall immigration and refugee policies, further enforcement funding would be throwing good money after bad."

An Enforcement-Only Approach Will Not Solve the Immigration Problem

Donald Kerwin and Robert Warren

In the following viewpoint, Donald Kerwin and Robert Warren argue that continued substantial increases in homeland security enforcement is not the solution to achieving the "effectiveness" rate, that is, the percentage of immigrants caught or returned. Furthermore, increasing enforcement at the borders does not serve to attack the root of the problem, which is that many people come to the United States because they are fleeing life-threatening conditions in their homelands. Many people are so desperate to get away from the violence and poverty at home that they are willing to risk the consequences of entering the United States illegally. Donald Kerwin is executive director of the Center for Migration Studies. Robert Warren is senior visiting fellow at the Center for Migration Studies.

"Does the United States Need to Invest More in Border Enforcement? " by Donald Kerwin and Robert Warren, The Center for Migration Studies (CMS). Reprinted by permission.

As you read, consider the following questions:

1. What was INS's budget in 1990, compared to comparable agencies in 2018?
2. What conditions are migrants from the Northern Triangle of Central America fleeing?
3. Why do the authors state that human smugglers are a symptom of bad policies rather than a cause of humanitarian crises?

The Trump administration came into office at a time when illegal border crossings from Mexico had been reduced to one-fourth from their historic highs and the US undocumented population had been falling for a decade. At present, the administration enjoys the largest immigration enforcement budget in US history, but in fiscal year (FY) 2019 the Department of Homeland Security (DHS) is on track to apprehend the highest numbers of border crossers in more than a decade. In both March and April, the Border Patrol recorded more than 100,000 apprehensions at the US-Mexico border. Its border enforcement strategies are failing on their own terms and, until the United States reassesses its overall immigration and refugee policies, further enforcement funding would be throwing good money after bad.

Customs and Border Protection (CBP) needs increased staffing and better infrastructure at certain ports of entry (POEs), where large quantities of illegal narcotics enter the country and illegal firearms and drug proceeds leave it. It may also need to expand its capacity to respond in real time to changed migration patterns. However, lack of resources does not explain the administration's failures. Rather, it is its failure to respond adequately to the conditions driving Central American and (increasingly) Venezuelan migrants, to provide legal pathways to protection for those fleeing violence and other impossible conditions, and to create a strong, well-resourced US asylum system.[1]

Historically Unprecedented Immigration Enforcement Spending

In 1990, the total appropriation to the Immigration and Naturalization Service (INS)—for both immigration enforcement and adjudication of applications—was $1.2 billion. By 2018, the enacted budgets of the two DHS immigration enforcement agencies, CBP and Immigration and Customs Enforcement (ICE), equaled a combined $23.8 billion (DHS 2019, 21, 27). This figure does not include the significant immigration enforcement responsibilities and expenditures of: (1) US Citizenship and Immigration Services (USCIS), which primarily adjudicates immigration applications; (2) the Department of State (DOS), the Department of Justice (DOJ), and other federal agencies; (3) the federal criminal justice system, which prosecutes and adjudicates a high volume of illegal entry and re-entry offenses (TRAC 2017, 2018); and (4) the many states and localities officially delegated by ICE to enforce US immigration laws through programs like 287(g) (ICE 2018). While enforcement expenditures have increased, investments in the USCIS Asylum Corps and the Immigration Court system have lagged badly behind, leading to massive case backlogs and long delays in adjudicating cases (Kerwin 2018).

The president's budget for 2020 would increase combined CBP and ICE funding to $30.2 billion (DHS 2019, 21, 27). Moreover, the Trump administration has set "operational control"—defined as "the prevention of all unlawful entries"[2]—as its overarching border enforcement goal and metric. Because unattainable, this goal positions the administration to argue that border enforcement resources—however much they are increased—do not suffice, and to respond to its own failures by insisting on additional enforcement funding and ever more divisive and cruel enforcement tactics, like separating children from their parents.

According to a study by the Migration Policy Institute, the funding and staffing levels of CBP and ICE exceed the combined levels of the four major DOJ law enforcement agencies (Meissner et al. 2013). These two agencies also receive many times more in funding than the three main US labor standards and workplace protection entities and all the state labor standards agencies combined.

The Changed Composition of Border Crossers, the Diminishing US Unauthorized Population, and the Border Wall

On February 15, 2019, the President declared a national emergency at the US-Mexico border which, if it withstands legal scrutiny, will allow the administration to redirect an estimated $8 billion appropriated for other purposes, primarily from the Department of Defense, to extending the wall at the US-Mexico border. The proposed increases follow years of dramatically reduced arrivals across the border that have transformed the US undocumented population.

Apprehensions at the border—which include multiple entries of the same person—dropped from more than 1.6 million in 2000 to about 300,000 in 2017 even though the size of the Border Patrol more than doubled, from 9,200 in 2000 to 19,400 in 2017 (CBP 2017a,b). Between 2010 and 2017, the total undocumented population fell from 11,725,000 to 10,665,000, spurred by a 1.3 million decrease in the number of Mexican undocumented residents (Warren 2019). Moreover, since 2010 the number of persons that illegally crossed has been roughly one-half of the number that entered legally and overstayed their visas, undermining the case for a border wall (ibid.).

Beginning in FY 2014 and continuing through FY 2019, immense numbers of unaccompanied children and families, primarily from the Northern Triangle states of Central America, have been driven to the United States, Mexico, and elsewhere by some of the world's highest homicide rates, rampant extortion and conscription by gangs, criminal impunity, and intense poverty (Labrador and Renwick 2018). The number of migrants from Venezuela—a country in economic free fall and with very high rates of violent crime—has also increased sharply in recent years.

BORDER WALL NOT WORTH THE PRICE, STUDY SAYS

Researchers embarked on the study in the summer of 2016 after seeing a need for more empirical evidence on the effects of the border wall amid ongoing debates over immigration.

"Overall, we find that the additional fencing had a very small effect on migration and an overall negative effect on the economy," says Melanie Morten, an assistant professor of economics and faculty fellow at the Stanford Institute for Economic Policy Research (SIEPR).

"The wall was expensive to US taxpayers—they paid roughly $7 per person—but saw little to no economic benefits as a result. Some even saw their welfare fall," Morten says.

The wall did not significantly curtail migration, the researchers say. Using data from Mexican consulates on the flow of adult Mexican citizens who migrated between 2006 and 2010, the researchers estimated that the wall expansion reduced the total number of Mexican-born workers coming into the United States by only 0.6 percent, roughly 83,000 people.

Further analysis showed that the expansion of the wall largely harmed American workers. College-educated US workers lost an equivalent of $4.35 in annual income, while less-educated US workers benefited on average by only 36 cents. Taken together, "the costs far outweigh the benefits, even for low-skilled workers in the US," Morten says.

"Border Wall Came at High Cost, Low Benefit for U.S. Workers," by Stanford, Futurity, November 21, 2018.

Honduras, Venezuela, El Salvador, and Guatemala rank among the nations with world's highest intentional homicide rates at 1st, 2nd, 5th, and 6th respectively (World Atlas 2018). Many of these migrants have sought asylum in the United States, but mostly they are seeking protection wherever they can find it. They do not try to evade detection, but present themselves to Border Patrol agents or to CBP officials at POEs. CBP adds them to its "apprehension" statistics, as if they were criminals, but they have the legal right to seek asylum under both domestic and international law.

Enforcement-Only Approaches Are Counterproductive

Notwithstanding its extraordinary border enforcement budget, the Trump administration has presided over the highest numbers of border crossers in a decade. After peaking in 2000 and with the exception of a slight surge in FY 2014, arrests at the US-Mexico border were at or below 400,000 between 2011 and 2018. Over the first six months of FY 2019, however, Border Patrol apprehensions spiked to more than 361,000 (CBP 2019). Additional enforcement funding will do nothing to address the humanitarian crises compelling hundreds of thousands of persons to seek protection for themselves and their children, however slim the odds of finding it.

Human smugglers should not be viewed as a cause of this crisis, but as a symptom of bad policies. Some smugglers commit unspeakable acts. Others do not and enjoy the trust of members of migrant-sending communities. In any event, migrants mostly understand the risks of migrating and do not make decisions based solely on what smuggling facilitators tell them. Dr. Gabriella Sanchez, Migrant Smuggling Research Fellow at the European University Institute, reports that potential migrants "gather as much information as they can from friends, family members, clergy, media, and smugglers themselves, and make their decisions based on what they learn." Moreover, they are not cavalier about their children's safety. They are willing to subject themselves to greater risks than they would others, particularly their loved ones (Slack and Martinez 2018).

By all accounts, the administration's policies have been a boon to smugglers. The administration has failed to provide legal avenues for the truly desperate to reach protection, both persons fleeing violence and formerly deported persons seeking to return to their US families.[3] Instead, it has erected new barriers to the US asylum system, separated parents from their children at the border, enacted unsustainable and cruel "zero tolerance" criminal prosecution policies for asylum seekers and other border crossers, and terminated the Central American Minors (CAM) program which allowed El Salvadoran, Guatemalan, and Honduran children to undergo refugee screening in their own countries and, if approved, to join their legally present parents living in United States as refugees or parolees. At a time of record numbers of refugees worldwide, it has limited refugee admissions to the lowest number in the history of the US Refugee Assistance Program and sought to eviscerate the Temporary Protected Status (TPS) program, which allows designated national groups who cannot safely return home to remain in the United States.

These actions have been accompanied by the President's threats to end foreign aid to Mexico, El Salvador, Guatemala, and Honduras for "doing nothing" to stop migration to the United States, his repeated promises to enact ever "tougher" enforcement policies, and by his poisonous anti-immigrant rhetoric. With no legal options to migrate, little hope that conditions will improve in their home communities, and assurance (by the US president) that US policies will become more severe—most recently through threats to charge fees to apply for asylum, to deny bond and work authorization to asylum seekers, or to accelerate court hearings—large numbers have chosen not to wait at home (Wasem 2019). More border enforcement funding will do nothing to change this dynamic.

Conclusion

The United Nations High Commissioner for Refugees (UNHCR) reported that in 2017 there were 68.5 million forcibly displaced persons, including 25.4 million refugees (UNHCR 2018); that developing regions hosted 85 percent of them; and that increasing numbers of asylum seekers were fleeing Northern Central America and Venezuela (UNHCR 2018, 7, 40). These trends have grown more acute in the interim. On December 17, 2018, UN member states—albeit not the United States—affirmed the Global Compact on Refugees (GCR), which seeks to support communities in developing states that host refugees, promote refugee self-reliance, expand their legal access to third countries, and allow for their safe and dignified return home (UNGA 2019, § 7). Not all of the migrants from the Northern Triangle states of Central America, Venezuela, or other global hotspots meet the narrow refugee definition, but very high percentages of them have been forced from their homes by unsafe and untenable conditions.

The United States would be well served by the kind of holistic strategy and commitments promoted by the GCR. The nation's current enforcement-only approach will not improve conditions so that refugees and others at risk can stay or return home. Nor will it support their safe resettlement in other communities, afford them fair and timely asylum hearings, or allow them to reach safety through legal channels. It will make this humanitarian crisis worse, and do nothing to stop desperate people from crossing borders.

Notes

1. Although not the subject of this essay, many scholars and lawyers have also reported on the immense population of deportees from the United States that plan to return to their US families (Kerwin, Alulema, and Nicholson 2018) despite the risk of prosecution, detention, and removal. One study concluded that US immigration enforcement programs will inevitably fail "when placed against the powerful pull of family and home" (Martinez, Slack, and Martinez-Schuldt 2018).
2. Border Security and Immigration Enforcement Improvements, Exec. Order No. 13767, 82 Fed. Reg. 8793 (Jan. 25, 2017).
3. Of course, in any large-scale migrant flow, there will be persons with different intentions and motivations, making screening a necessity.

References

CBP (US Customs and Border Protection). 2017a. " Southwest Border Sectors: Total Illegal Alien Apprehensions by Fiscal Year (Oct. 1st through Sept. 30th)." Washington, DC: CBP. https://www.cbp.gov/sites/default/files/assets/documents/2017-Dec/BP%20Southwest%20Border%20Sector%20Apps%20FY1960%20-%20FY2017.pdf.

———. 2017b. "US Border Patrol Fiscal Year Staffing Statistics (FY 1992 - FY 2017)." Washington, DC: CBP. https://www.cbp.gov/document/stats/us-border-patrol-fiscal-year-staffing-statistics-fy-1992-fy-2017.

———. 2019. "US Border Patrol Southwest Border Apprehensions FY 2019." Washington, DC: CBP. https://www.cbp.gov/newsroom/stats/sw-border-migration.

DHS (US Department of Homeland Security). 2019. FY 2020 Budget in Brief. Washington, DC: DHS. https://www.dhs.gov/sites/default/files/publications/19_0318_MGMT_FY-2020-Budget-In-Brief.pdf.

ICE (US Immigration and Customs Enforcement). 2018. "Delegation of Immigration Authority Section 287(g) Immigration and Nationality Act." Washington, DC: ICE. https://www.ice.gov/287g.

Kerwin, Donald. 2018. "From IIRIRA to Trump: Connecting the Dots to the Current US Immigration Policy Crisis." Journal on Migration and Human Security 6(3): 192-204.   https://doi.org/10.1177/2331502418786718.

Kerwin, Donald, Daniela Alulema, and Mike Nicholson. 2018. "Communities in Crisis: Interior Removals and their Human Consequences." Journal on Migration and Human Security 6(4): 226-42. https://doi.org/10.1177/2331502418820066.

Labrador, Rocio Cara, and Danielle Renwick. 2018. "Central America's Violent Northern Triangle." Backgrounder. New York: Council on Foreign Relations. https://www.cfr.org/backgrounder/central-americas-violent-northern-triangle.

Martinez, Daniel E., Jeremy Slack, and Ricardo D. Martinez-Schuldt. 2018. "Repeat Migration in the Age of the 'Unauthorized Permanent Resident': A Quantitative Assessment of Migration Intentions Postdeportation." International Migration Review 52(4): 1186-217. https://doi.org/10.1177/0197918318767921.

Meissner, Doris, Donald Kerwin, Muzaffar Chishti, and Claire Bergeron. 2013. "Immigration Enforcement in the United States: the Rise of a Formidable Machinery." Washington, DC: Migration Policy Institute. https://www.migrationpolicy.org/research/immigration-enforcement-united-states-rise-formidable-machinery.

Slack, Jeremy, and Daniel E. Martinez. 2018. "What Makes a Good Human Smuggler? The Differences between Satisfaction with and Recommendations of Coyotes on the US-Mexico Border." The Annals of the American Academy of Political and Social Science 676(1): 152-73. https://doi.org/10.1177/0002716217750562.

TRAC (Transactional Records Access Clearinghouse. 2017. "Criminal Immigration Prosecutions Down 14% in FY 2017." Syracuse, NY: TRAC. http://trac.syr.edu/tracreports/crim/494/.

———. 2018. "Stepped Up Illegal-Entry Prosecutions Reduce Those for Other Crimes." Syracuse NY: TRAC. https://trac.syr.edu/immigration/reports/524/.

UNGA (United National General Assembly). 2018. Report of the United Nations High Commissioner for Refugees: Part II Global Compact on Refugees. UN Doc. A/73/12 (Part II). New York, NY: United Nations. https://reliefweb.int/sites/reliefweb.int/files/resources/5b3295167.pdf.

UNHCR (United Nations High Commissioner for Refugees). 2018. Global Trends: Forced Displacement in 2017. Geneva: UNHCR. https://www.unhcr.org/5b27be547.pdf.

Warren, Robert. 2019. "US Undocumented Population Continued to Fall from 2016 to 2017 and Visa Overstays Significantly Exceeded Illegal Crossings for the Seventh Consecutive Year." Journal on Migration and Human Security 6(1): 1-4. https://doi.org/10.1177/2331502419830339.

Wasem, Ruth Ellen. 2019. "To solve the US 'crisis at the border,' look to its cause." The Hill, April 4. https://thehill.com/opinion/immigration/436725-to-solve-the-us-crisis-at-the-border-look-to-its-cause.

World Atlas. 2018. "Murder Rate by Country." https://www.worldatlas.com/articles/murder-rates-by-country.html.

> *"Many parents reported they were pressured into giving up their right to reunify with their children, being forced to sign documents without asking questions and punished with solitary confinement and starvation for raising concerns or simply being distraught at the unknown fate of their kin."*

Immigrant Families Are Separated by Trump Policies

Tasnim News Agency

In the following viewpoint, the staff of the Tasnim News Agency reports on the failure of the Trump administration to act quickly in reuniting families separated at the border. A US District Court judge ruled there is no legal reason for immigrant families to face separation from each other. The separation is caused by the detention of immigrant adults, leaving the children—some under the age of five—alone. These children then became the custody of the government. As reported, even those families who had been reunited faced long-term trauma from the separation. The Tasnim News Agency is a private news organization based in Iran that covers political and international subjects.

As you read, consider the following questions:

1. How could trauma linger even after reuniting parents with their children, according to the viewpoint?
2. Why are immigrants' rights activists calling for reparations after the separations?
3. What is the problem with putting detained children with foster families according to the viewpoint?"

I t's been almost two months since a US judge ordered the US government to reunite immigrant children separated from their parents at the border, but hundreds remain apart.

Meantime, hundreds remain apart as news spreads that parents have been deported while their children were in custody and that reunited young children don't recognize their parents any more.

The June 26 preliminary injunction issued by US District Court Judge Dana Sabraw in California gave the federal government 14 days to reunite children under five years of age with their parents and 30 days to reunite the rest; twice that time has passed, and according to an ACLU joint status report filed with Immigration and Customs Enforcement (ICE) on August 16, 565 children remain apart from their parents and in government custody, Sputnik reported.

Of those children, 366, including six who are under the age of five, have had their parents deported to their home countries in that time. Another 203 not included in the 565 were released from government detention without being reunited with their parents, including 19 under the age of five. Those children may have been released to a relative or family friend or may have turned 18 while in custody, CNN noted.

However, to date, 1,923 children have been reunited with their families as of Thursday.

"There's real progress being made and real effort being made in some of these home countries, Guatemala and Honduras," Judge Sabraw said in court Friday. "[It] looks or is very encouraging, at least, that everything is being done to locate as many of these parents as can be. So the report would indicate to the court that the efforts on the ground are productive and certainly heading in the right direction."

But even those reunions can be traumatizing, and it's clear that major psychological damage has been done, especially to younger children. One heart-rending video posted by the ACLU on its Twitter account shows a mother and child reunited, but when the mother embraces her son, he pulls away from her as she sobs, "I'm your mommy… what's wrong with my son?"

In a new complaint filed with the US Department of Homeland Security by the American Immigration Lawyers Association on Thursday, civil rights advocates allege that DHS officials coerced, degraded, threatened and punished parents after taking away their children.

Many parents reported they were pressured into giving up their right to reunify with their children, being forced to sign documents without asking questions and punished with solitary confinement and starvation for raising concerns or simply being distraught at the unknown fate of their kin, Vice reported.

"Together these practices have resulted in not only the tremendous suffering of children and parents who have been kept apart, detained and subjected to abusive, inhumane treatment, but also the involuntary, forced return of hundreds of people to grave dangers, including risk of death," the complaint reads.

Sputnik Radio's Loud & Clear spoke Friday with Juan Carlos Ruiz, cofounder of the New Sanctuary Coalition, about the continually delayed reunification of families and what it signifies.

"Right from the start… this administration did not intend to reunify our families," the activist told hosts Brian Becker and John Kiriakou. "This is evidence of that. This is psychological torture. This is practically breaking international law, and it's a clear message to our communities, a message of terrorizing our communities, of basically saying they have the power to disappear our loved ones, not to reunite the children with their parents. It's an act of cruelty. I have never seen this level of cruelty visited upon our communities. I've been fighting within the immigrant rights movement for over 20 years, and I've never seen this evil around us. We have a whole system already that is established and well-oiled that separates our children from their families, from their parents, but this level of cruelty hasn't been accomplished until now."

"They have kids who are six years old, basically saying 'that woman' [while] pointing to their mothers, after being separated for two months, two months and a half. We still have parents that are in detention centers, and we know where their kids are, and they are not being allowed to be united. But these kids are angry; these kids do not understand what is going on, and you are right on when you say the damage has already been done," the activist pointed out.

"We have to talk about reparations. We have to talk about acknowledging the intention of this government, the… world that is already well-established, backed up by a system, by a whole apparatus of Homeland Security that has the intention of continuing to terrorize our communities."

"There is nothing humane about this. It's really a wall of hatred, a wall of racism, a wall that terrorizes our communities and that is well-established and in place."

Ruiz noted that the Border Patrol has the full power and discretion not to deport parents while their children remain in US custody, but chooses not to. "This is the work of not just one person; it is a whole system that is set up to do this… We need full accountability, full transparency. We need those people who have made these declarations — irresponsible declarations — to really pay up the consequences. This is a crime, nothing less than a crime. This is cruelty against our humanity — our common humanity, you know, not just the people."

"I think we need to account for that; we need to pay up; we need to do reparations. Our families who are being reunited, they are being practically abandoned. They are being practically left to their own means, after such a traumatizing experience, so we need to denounce that also. Here in New York, at the Cayuga Center, we don't know how many kids we still have in our facilities here. There is no monetary—remember, these are mostly agencies that work without any checks and balances—"

The Cayuga Center is a private company in the New York City area, one of seven centers that does foster care for immigrant children.

"They get the children, and they place them… they are asking for families to come and adopt—kind of adopt, foster a child. They have psychological service for them. They have… care services, children care," the activist said.

Ruiz noted the major financial incentives behind families seeking to foster immigrant children."They vet families who can take the kids home, and they pay them… $1,000 per month. Given the high demand, some families got 12 kids, eight kids per family; some of the families were not vetted."

"What kind of a country does this?" Ruiz asked. "Who are we before the international community?"

> "It's hard to put a price tag on the
> benefits of achieving the 'American
> Dream.'"

Republicans, If You Want to Stop Immigration, Think About Economics

Thomas More Smith

In the following viewpoint, Thomas More Smith argues that Republication immigration policies ignore the economic benefits of immigration. He examines the potential costs of a hypothetical Mexican construction worker relative to the benefits of this worker's immigration. He concludes that it is in the worker's best economic interest to cross the border. Therefore, if the Republicans want to deter immigration from Mexico, they need to alter the economic advantages so immigration appears far less attractive. Thomas More Smith is an economist and finance professor at Emory University's Goizueta Business School in Atlanta, Georgia.

As you read, consider the following questions:

1. What is the E-verify system?
2. What role does a "coyote" serve?
3. In what ways should Republicans change the benefits calculation?

Two of the top GOP presidential contenders each claim professional creds that trump political experience (pun intended).

Trump's empire, according to him, has a net worth of US$10 billion and is the only line on his CV that counts. "If you can run a huge business, you can run a country," he seems to be saying.

Carly Fiorina seems to be claiming the same thing as she touts her experience as the CEO of Hewlett-Packard (though some might add "into the ground" to that first phrase).

Both of these candidates (and every other Republican candidate) has an opinion on how to curb/reduce/eliminate undocumented immigrants. Given the business experience of the top candidates, their strategies for handling the issue are puzzling. "Let's build a higher wall—and have Mexico pay for it." "Let's eliminate birth-right citizenship." "Let's use technology to rid the US of undocumented immigrants."

These policies fail to meet the standards of Business 101 because they ignore the cost-benefit equation of immigration. Here's how.

What's the Equation?

If a business owner, business strategist or chief operations officer is able to understand the marginal costs of an action relative to its marginal benefits, she or he can make better decisions. That is, the company should build the next unit only if, all things being equal, the marginal benefit exceeds the marginal cost.

Trump likely does such economic analyses all the time (or hires others to do it). He knows well that a core tenet of economics and finance is that capital earns a return and thus should be allocated to earn the highest one possible.

We see this play out in the market all the time. The owner of an acre of land will use it to maximize revenue, by building a skyscraper instead of a one-story convenience store or constructing condos rather than office space.

More Than Eleven Million Unauthorized Immigrants Live in America

There were 11.1 million unauthorized immigrants living in the U.S. in March 2011, unchanged from the previous two years and a continuation of the sharp decline in this population since its peak in 2007, according to estimates by the Pew Hispanic Center, a project of the Pew Research Center.

As the Pew Hispanic Center reported earlier this year, net immigration from Mexico to the United States has stopped and possibly reversed through 2010. At its peak in 2000, about 770,000 immigrants arrived annually from Mexico; the majority arrived illegally. By 2010, the inflow had dropped to about 140,000—a majority of whom arrived as legal immigrants, according to Pew Hispanic Center estimates.

In addition, the number of Mexicans and their children who moved from the U.S. to Mexico between 2005 and 2010 roughly doubled from the number who had done so in the five-year period a decade before.

"Unauthorized Immigrants: 11.1 Million in 2011," by Jeffrey S. Passel and D'vera Cohn, Pew Research Center, December 6, 2012.

Although the example above regards physical capital, these same decisions are made with human capital. For example, The Donald commands $100,000 or more to deliver a speech. So what's the best use of his time? He hires a bunch of economists and finance gurus to run the numbers on prospective deals while he spends more time talking because he receives a higher return for public appearances (and continues to increase the value of his "brand").

The Numbers in the Equation

Let's imagine another Donald. Not the real estate mogul we know, but rather his Mexican namesake, a construction worker, who wasn't born into wealth and power.

The average monthly salary for construction laborers in Mexico is the equivalent of $235. The average monthly wage for a construction worker in the US is $2,499. This comparison is lopsided for any number of professions, from university professors ($827 v $5,747) to police officers ($670 v $4,734), according to federal statistical data from both countries.

The Mexican Donald interested in emigrating north asks the following question: "Is it worth it for me to cross the border into the US?" He assumes the benefit is higher wages—approximately $2,264 more per month. But what are the costs?

We start counting the costs by assuming that we are talking about sneaking across the US border, since the odds of securing a legal way across are relatively slim.

The costs of immigrating can be divided among those that are explicit, implicit and tied to opportunity. The explicit costs include, for example, hiring a truck to transport you from one location to another, while the implicit costs include the disconnection from community or family when moving from an originating location to a new destination. Opportunity costs include any lost wages incurred while the move is taking place or lost productivity as a result of being in a new market or having skill sets that do not immediately translate into productive work.

An undocumented Mexican Donald, sneaking across the border into California or New Mexico, for example, will have the direct costs of a "coyote" (guide) and other direct costs associated with trekking from one country to another (food, clothing, shelter, transportation and identification), and indirect costs associated with removal from one community and insertion into another, and, of course, the costs associated with the possibility of assault, sexual assault or murder.

These costs can vary from several hundred to multiple thousands of dollars. A quick smuggle from Tijuana, for example, might cost $500, while a trek from Southern Mexico might run upwards of $10,000.

Table 1 illustrates these costs for a Mexican immigrant from a town/area within 500 miles of the US border requiring five days and nights to get to the border and a five-day stay at a stash house once across the border.

Table 1: Costs of Migration

ITEM	APPROXIMATE COST
Guide	$550
Lodging/day (x5)	$11.50
Bribes: Gangs	$100
Bribes: Police	$400
Bribes: Drug Cartel	$275
Driver	$175
Boatmen	$100
Stash house/day (x5)	$20
Identification	$100
Total	$1,857.50

Source: Daily Mail

The Cost-Benefit Analysis

In order for someone to migrate from Mexico to the US, he or she must identify that the stream of benefits (wages) net of all the costs (direct and indirect) is greater than the benefits of staying in place.

In the scenario suggested, we have a construction worker who will have a wage differential of approximately $2,264 per month and would clear about $280 a month after living expenses. This immigrant will make the move as long as he has a strong belief that he will be staying in the US for at least a year or two.

And, if he thinks he will stay for five years, he has a positive net present value of $12,712, assuming he saves that $280 every month during the first year and increases savings by 3% each subsequent year. The net present value, as you might recall, is a calculation that converts future benefits into present benefits. Considering that the wage for this person is $235 per month in Mexico, even if he were able to save $100 per month it would have taken 127 months, or nearly 10.5 years to accumulate the same amount of money. Under these assumptions, the cost-benefit analysis suggests the person should come to the US.

Changing the Calculation

So how do Trump's and other Republicans' policies change the calculation? Building higher walls (or electric fences? per Fiorina's technology push) and removing naturalized citizen status might increase the costs of immigrating.

Obviously, higher walls are harder to climb. But, given that crossing deserts brings a slow miserable death to a number of these immigrants (and others will suffocate in the back of cargo trucks or be murdered by smugglers), a few more feet to climb is probably going to deter only a small number of potential immigrants.

Repealing the 14th amendment, which provides US citizenship to anyone born here, might decrease the stream of benefits. This benefit was not included in the analysis above. If I had included this, the stream of benefits would outweigh the costs by even more, though it would be difficult to put a value on what it's worth to a Mexican mother or father.

However, the data reveal that the number of foreign-born Mexican women giving birth in the last 12 months (presumably within the US) is only 7% of all foreign-born women Mexican immigrants. Removing this "benefit" directly affect only 400,000 of more than 11.3 million foreign-born Mexican immigrants in the US. That is, it is a benefit that doesn't affect a huge share of the immigrant population at large.

So What if Trump Wanted to Change the Calculation?

If these "business" candidates for president want to reduce or eliminate undocumented immigrants, they have to tackle this problem from the benefit side.

The benefits used in the calculation assume that the immigrant will have a 100% chance of landing a job at the going wage. But that's not the case in Arizona, which requires businesses to use E-verify, a system in which businesses electronically verify that the documentation presented by a potential employee has matching information between the name and the social security number (securing proof of eligibility to work). That's a big hurdle that gives an undocumented immigrants a much smaller chance at landing a job.

Whether it's a good policy or not, if more states adopted systems like E-verify, the cost-benefit calculation for immigrants from Latin America would look decidedly grimmer for the immigrant. If the chances of finding a job become very small, it would become much harder to justify making the treacherous trek (the costs would out weight the benefits).

All the same, like the value of giving your child US citizenship, it's hard to put a price tag on the benefits of achieving the "American Dream." This suggests that no matter what policy Trump or others pursue to increase the cost of immigration, it will be hard pressed to work as long as the US remains the proverbial "land of opportunity."

> "*Deportations and detentions of non-citizens often negatively impact U.S. citizens because undocumented immigrants do not live separate and walled-off lives from the documented, but instead live side by side in the same communities and in the same families.*"

Open Borders Would Help Immigrants and Americans

Joel Newman

In the following viewpoint Joel Newman argues that immigration restrictions hurt not only the immigrants, but also Americans. An advocate for open borders, Newman contends that because immigrants are integrated into society, other Americans suffer when they are harassed, detained, and deported as a result of strict immigration policies. Businesses, families, and communities would benefit from an open border policy, the author maintains. Joel Newman has a bachelor's degree in history from Pomona College and works as a teacher in Beaverton, Oregon.

"Immigration Restrictions Hurt Americans Too," by Joel Newman, Open Borders, August 23, 2017. Retrieved from https://openborders.info/blog/immigration-restrictions-hurt-americans/ Licensed under CC BY 3.0 Unported.

As you read, consider the following questions:

1. What did the ACLU call the US southern border, largely because of practices such as those enforced by Arizona sheriff Joe Arpaio?
2. How can US citizens be mistaken for noncitizens and deported?
3. How can immigration enforcement hurt US businesses, according to the viewpoint?

American immigration restrictions inflict immense suffering on immigrants and would-be immigrants. Thousands have died attempting to enter the U.S. through the desert, and others have perished attempting to make sea journeys. Tens of thousands languish each year in detention centers. Others are abused by government agents or criminals. Many are deported from the U.S. after having lived many years here. Millions of undocumented immigrants live anxious lives, not knowing if or when they will be arrested and deported.

Another group is also harmed by the restrictions: American citizens. Like immigrants, they suffer in myriad ways.

To begin with, Latino citizens sometimes must endure profiling by authorities seeking undocumented immigrants. NBC News notes that "Latino and immigrant groups say that due to increased enforcement, being Latino in some places is enough to be pulled over under the guise of a minor traffic stop and be asked to prove American citizenship." Several years ago Sheriff Joe Arpaio in Arizona (who is no longer sheriff) was ordered by a judge to cease stopping people to check their immigration status because the stops amounted to racial profiling. And "the ACLU, border-town residents, members of Congress and even some border patrol agents argue that the rapid and vast expansion of immigration enforcement in the years since the Department of Homeland Security was created, without expanded oversight to match it, has turned the southern border of the U.S. into an occupied police state, where abuses of power and harassment by agents are an everyday occurrence."

Some American citizens actually have been detained and perhaps deported by immigration authorities. Over the last decade hundreds of U.S.. citizens have been detained, either at local jails at the request of immigration officials or at immigration detention centers, even though immigration agents do not have the authority to detain citizens. One citizen was imprisoned for over three years because he was mistakenly considered to be a non-citizen. Another spent almost two years in detention. One researcher suggests that some citizens have actually been deported in recent years. Looking further back in history, probably hundreds of thousands of citizens of Mexican descent were deported to Mexico in the 1920s and 1930s.

In addition, deportations and detentions of non-citizens often negatively impact U.S. citizens. This is because, in the words of a report by the Center for American Progress, "undocumented immigrants do not live separate and walled-off lives from the documented, but instead live side by side in the same communities and in the same families." It is estimated that about 4 million children who are citizens have one or more undocumented parents, and The Washington Post reports that more than 100,000 citizens lose a spouse or parent to deportation each year.

Deportations separate citizen children from parents and, for families who have not yet experienced deportation, create fear among children that they could be separated from their parents in the future. Detentions also are traumatizing for children. For example, after a father of two U.S. citizens had been in detention for six months, his wife reported that "her 2-year-old son wakes up crying for his father every night, while her 3-year-old daughter has refused to learn to count or tie her shoes until he comes home." Citizen children also experience raids on homes by immigration agents.

Adult U.S. citizens, like citizen children, suffer when immigration enforcement targets family members. In one case, an American wife of a man facing deportation was diagnosed with situational depression after he was detained. Another American wife accompanied her husband when he was deported but wanted to be able to return to the U.S. with him and their child, stating "'We do not have any family or friends here (London). We are all on our own… We desperately want to come home.'"

Immigration enforcement also hurts many U.S. businesses. Farmers sometimes can't find enough workers to harvest their crops because of immigration restrictions. Different kinds of firms suffer if their workers are deported. Businesses can be punished for hiring undocumented workers.

At the same time, citizen workers in some cases may endure poor working conditions because employers, using the threat of reporting undocumented coworkers to immigration authorities, can stifle efforts to unionize or report labor violations. As one article noted, "immigrants' inability to invoke their rights results in weakened employment protections for all American workers— and in some instances, means that American workers are subject to violations of minimum-wage and overtime protections, wage theft, and other forms of employment violations, such as unsafe working conditions." In 2009 the AFL-CIO and other organizations reported that

> One of the most devastating illegal employer tactics is the threat to call immigration authorities on workers. The chilling impact of employers' unlawful threats is felt not only by undocumented workers, but by their co-workers. Documented workers and U.S. citizens may be reluctant to organize their workplaces because properly timed threats to turn workers over to immigration authorities can undermine the union election process. And if workers should win a union election, deportation of their undocumented co-workers will dilute the power of the bargaining unit. No industry relies solely on an immigrant workforce. The Census Bureau's 2007 American Community Survey found that of more than 330 occupations, only two have immigrant majorities. This means that threats

to call immigration authorities deprive workers in nearly every industry of their right to a voice at work.

Open borders would end all of this suffering endured by so many American citizens. Citizen spouses and children wouldn't have to worry about or experience the arrest, detention, and deportation of a loved family member. Citizens themselves wouldn't be detained or deported. Workers' efforts to report labor violations or organize wouldn't be undermined by immigration enforcement, and businesses could depend on a free flow of needed labor. Open borders would benefit immigrants and citizens alike.

> "*The fact that economic inequality is 'the most robust predictor of border walls' indicates that walls built in recent decades were designed to fortify countries against unwanted immigrants and illegal trade.*"

What the Research Says About Border Walls

Denise-Marie Ordway

In the following viewpoint Denise-Marie Ordway examines the research available on border walls. The author notes that the number of border barriers worldwide has increased considerably in the last 30 years, despite the fact that experts question their effectiveness and negative impact on economies, population, and the environment. She rounds up several key sources for an exploration into this topic. Denise-Marie Ordway writes for Journalist's Resource. Her work also has appeared in USA Today, *the* New York Times, *and* Washington Post, *among other publications.*

As you read, consider the following questions:

1. How many border barriers are there around the world, according to the viewpoint?
2. According to the viewpoint, what is the connection between border walls and economies?
3. How do border walls impact the environment, according to the viewpoint?

As American lawmakers argue over whether to fund a wall along the United States' southwestern border, the federal government has moved ahead with plans to replace some of the fencing it built there years ago with a 30-foot-tall steel bollard wall. Meanwhile, a growing number of countries worldwide have built border walls and other barriers to try to control the flow of people and goods.

There are a total of about 70 border barriers worldwide, Elisabeth Vallet, director of the Center for Geopolitical Studies at the University of Quebec-Montreal, told Journalist's Resource. Her research demonstrates how popular these structures have become—there were about 15 of them in 1990. Vallet is one of a number of scholars in the field who have spoken out against man-made barriers, arguing they are expensive and dangerous and questioning their effectiveness. Several of those scholars weighed in with essays published in a recent issue of the Journal of Latin American Geography.

Here in the U.S., the Department of Homeland Security (DHS) has erected more than 650 miles of fence and other types of barrier along the almost 2,000-mile U.S.-Mexico border. Even before President Donald Trump took office, federal law required the barrier to be expanded by another almost 50 miles. In December, DHS announced that it had completed most of a $292 million project to build 40 miles of steel wall to replace "an outdated and operationally ineffective barrier" in the San Diego, El Centro and El Paso sectors of the border.

Lawmakers have until Feb. 15 to reach a compromise on a new border security plan or there could be another government shutdown. Disagreement over funding—Trump wants $5.7 billion in border wall money—led to a 35-day shutdown that ended Jan. 25, 2019.

To help journalists understand this issue and put it into context, we've pulled together academic studies, federal government reports and other scholarly literature. Below, we have summarized research that explains what border barriers are, why they have become so popular and whether they actually help countries control their borders. We have also included research that investigates the consequences of building these barriers, including impacts on the environment and local communities.

It's important to note that government officials, politicians, scholars and others tend to use the terms "fence," "wall" and "barrier" interchangeably when discussing man-man structures built to control a country's borders. There also is some confusion over terms such as "border security." New York Times reporter Glenn Thrush wrote an article offering a "glossary of the border debate."

Understanding Border Barriers

"Why Do States Build Walls? Political Economy, Security, and Border Stability"
Carter, David B.; Poast, Paul. Journal of Conflict Resolution, 2017.

This study looks at the reasons why governments in various parts of the world erected border walls between 1800 and 2014. They refer to border wall construction as a "particularly aggressive strategy" for addressing unauthorized crossings and explain that walls are "almost always evidence that neighbors are not effectively cooperating in managing the border and have inconsistent border management strategies."

The researchers examined 62 border walls, some of which stretch thousands of miles. France, Israel, Saudi Arabia and the

Soviet Union are "the most active users" of border walls, the authors note. In addition, more than half of border walls erected during the last two centuries were built in the post-Cold War era.

The researchers find that territorial disputes are not a consistent factor driving governments to erect walls. Neither is the presence of civil war in a neighboring state. Economic inequality, however, is. "Borders that separate economies with very different levels of development are likely to be unstable," the authors write. "This instability is associated with a significantly higher probability of wall construction."

According to the authors, the fact that economic inequality is "the most robust predictor of border walls" indicates that walls built in recent decades were designed to fortify countries against unwanted immigrants and illegal trade.

"Progress and Challenges with the Use of Technology, Tactical Infrastructure, and Personnel to Secure the Southwest Border"
Report of the U.S. Government Accountability Office, GAO-18-397T, March 2018.

This report examines some of the challenges the U.S. Customs and Border Protection (CBP) faces in using technology, border fencing and other resources to control the U.S.-Mexico border. The report, released by the U.S. Government Accountability Office, also criticizes the U.S. Customs and Border Protection and the Border Patrol for not doing more to assess the effectiveness of their efforts.

For example, the report notes that U.S. Customs and Border Protection "has not developed metrics that systematically use data it collects to assess the contributions of border fencing to its mission, as the Government Accountability Office has recommended." Also, the Border Patrol "has not yet used available data to determine the contribution of surveillance technologies to border security efforts."

The report spotlights problems in maintaining the border fence. "From fiscal years 2010 through 2015, CBP recorded a total of 9,287 breaches in pedestrian fencing, and repair costs averaged

$784 per breach," according to the report. Parts of the fence have become so degraded they needed replacing. From 2011 to 2016, CBP spent $4.84 million per mile, on average, to replace 14.1 miles of border fencing.

"Barriers Along the U.S. Borders: Key
Authorities and Requirements"
Garcia, Michael John. Report of the Congressional Research Center, March 2017.

This 44-page report, issued by Congress' public policy research arm, offers a close examination of the federal laws and policies that govern how physical barriers can or should be used along America's international borders. The report also outlines the various laws that DHS can waive for the construction of border fencing—the Safe Drinking Water Act, Archeological Resources Protection Act and the Migratory Bird Treaty Act, for example. In the report, Michael John Garcia, the acting section research manager for the Congressional Research Center, also makes it clear that there are no legal barriers to prevent the expansion of a America's border barrier.

Garcia explains that after several hundred miles of barrier were constructed between 2005 and 2011, DHS "largely stopped deploying additional fencing, as the agency altered its enforcement strategy in a manner that places less priority upon barrier construction." Before Trump became president in 2017, federal law already required DHS to build almost 50 miles of additional barrier. However, no deadline had been set for the completion of that expansion, according to the report.

Effectiveness, Economic Impacts

"Border Walls"
Allen, Treb; Dobbin, Cauê de Castro; Morten, Melanie. National Bureau of Economic Research Working Paper No. 25267, November 2018.

Scholars from Dartmouth College and Stanford University examine how expanding the U.S.-Mexico border fence has affected migration and the U.S. economy. They focus on the segment erected between 2007 and 2010 under the Secure Fence Act of 2006, which added 548 miles of reinforced fencing in Arizona, California, New Mexico, and Texas.

The key takeaway: The $2.3 billion project curbed migration and benefited low-skill U.S. workers but hurt high-skill U.S. workers. "In total, we estimate the Secure Fence Act reduced the aggregate Mexican population living in the United States by 0.64 percent, equivalent to a reduction of 82,647 people," the authors write.

Researchers find that for each migrant lost, America's gross domestic product fell by about $30,000. "Because the wall expansion resulted in fewer Mexican workers residing in the United States, economic activity was redistributed toward Mexico, increasing real GDP in Mexico by $1.2 billion and causing real GDP in the United States to fall by $2.5 billion," they write.

The expansion led to a slight increase in per capita income—an extra 36 cents—for low-skill workers in the U.S. Meanwhile, high-skill workers saw a small drop—an estimated loss of $4.35.

According to the analysis, another fence expansion "would have larger impacts on migration from Mexico to the United States, they would also result in greater reallocation of economic activity to Mexico; for example, a wall expansion that builds along half the remaining uncovered border would result in 144,256 fewer Mexican workers residing in the United States, causing the United States real GDP to decline by $4.3 billion, or approximately $29,800 in lost economic output for each migrant prevented."

It's important to note that the researchers' estimates are based on the number of Mexican citizens living in the U.S. who applied for an identification card from a Mexican consulate in the U.S. It is unclear what percentage of Mexican citizens residing in the U.S. seek a consulate ID card, about 850,000 of which are issued per year, according to the study.

The researchers suggest that instead of expanding the border fence, a better option for reducing migration would be to cut the costs of trade between the two countries. That should result in higher wages in Mexico, the authors explain. Cutting trade costs by 25 percent, for example, "would have resulted in both greater declines in Mexico to United States migration and substantial welfare gains for all workers."

Population Impacts
"Due Diligence and Demographic Disparities:
Effects of the Planning of U.S.-Mexico Border
Fence on Marginalized Populations"
Wilson, J. Gaines; et al. Southwestern Geographer, 2010.
This study, from researchers at several Texas universities, examines the "social justice impacts" of a DHS plan to erect border fence in certain parts of Texas. Researchers looked specifically at the plan outlined in the DHS' November 2007 Environmental Impact Statement for the Rio Grande Valley Sector. They focused on the path of the fence through Cameron County, Texas, comparing locations where the USDHS planned to erect fence and locations where they planned to leave gaps. They considered how the project would affect individuals' use and ownership of the land.

The authors find that the plan, which was later amended, would have had a disproportionate impact on people with lower incomes and education levels as well as Hispanics and people who were not U.S. citizens. The researchers note that it does not appear the federal government studied how the fence would affect communities before devising its plan. The DHS "did not show sufficient due diligence in understanding and mitigating any disparate impacts," the authors write, adding that DHS "acknowledged that the general placement of the fence along the Mexican border ensures that poor Hispanic immigrant families are those most likely to be affected by its construction."

The researchers write that although the fence route eventually changed, but they are not clear how it changed. The DHS "has not provided any information indicating that the route changed substantially or that the government considered the characteristics of those who were impacted in making changes to the location of the fence," they explain.

Environmental Impacts

"Border Fences and Their Impacts on Large Carnivores, Large Herbivores and Biodiversity: An International Wildlife Law Perspective" Trouwborst, Arie; Fleurke, Floor; Dubrulle, Jennifer. Review of European Comparative & International Environmental Law, 2016.

This article, which appears in an international law journal, examines border fences' impact on wildlife and natural habitats from an international law and policy perspective. The authors explain that the characteristics of each type of barrier affects wildlife differently. Existing barriers are made of a range of materials, including concrete, sand, barbed or razor wire and electrified fencing. In some cases, metal walls extend underground. Some fencing strategies involve land mines.

Barriers are of particular concern in Central Asia, home to a variety of migratory and nomadic mammals, the authors write. "By splitting populations, impeding migrations and killing animals attempting to cross, border fences pose an actual or potential threat to many of these, including the Mongolian gazelle (Procapra gutturosa), saiga antelope (Saiga tatarica), Asiatic wild ass (Equus hemionus, also known as khulan), Bactrian camel (Camelus ferus), argali sheep (Ovis ammon) and snow leopard (Panthera uncia)," they write.

The scholars point out that current laws and policies could be improved to prevent and ameliorate the impacts of border barriers worldwide. Barriers "have the potential to undo decades of conservation and international collaboration efforts, and their proliferation entails a need to realign our conservation paradigms with the political reality on the ground," they write.

"Nature Divided, Scientists United: US–Mexico Border Wall Threatens Biodiversity and Binational Conservation"
Peters, Robert; et al. BioScience, October 2018.

This call to action, which criticizes the U.S.-Mexico border barrier and Trump's proposed expansion of it, was signed by more than 2,500 scientists representing dozens of countries, including 1,472 from the U.S. and 616 from Mexico. It stresses the barrier's "negative impacts on wildlife, habitat, and binational collaboration in conservation and scientific research" and offers recommendations for limiting harm.

The authors explain that a continuous border wall or fence "could disconnect more than 34 percent of U.S. nonflying native terrestrial and freshwater animal species … from the 50 percent or more of their range that lies south of the border." They complain that the border barrier and security operations have obstructed scientific research. "U.S. and Mexican scientists have shared distressing stories of being intimidated, harassed, and delayed by border security officers," they write.

The scientists offer four recommendations for moving forward, the first of which is for Congress to make sure DHS follows federal environmental laws. "Any future appropriations for border barrier construction and operations should require adherence to all environmental laws and preclude their waiver," the authors write. "In areas where the DHS has already issued waivers, we call on the DHS to carry out analysis, mitigation, and opportunities for public participation as prescribed by all relevant environmental laws."

The remaining three recommendations focus on performing surveys to identify species and habitats at risk, avoiding barriers in areas with "high ecological sensitivity" and facilitating "scientific research in the borderlands to complement and assist environmental evaluation and mitigation efforts."

"Border Security Fencing and Wildlife: The End of the Transboundary Paradigm in Eurasia?"
Linnell, John D.C.; et al. PLOS Biology, June 2016.

In this peer-reviewed article, scientists from Europe and Asia offer their views on how wildlife are harmed by border fencing in Europe, the Caucasus and Central Asia. They specifically discuss the impact on bears, lynx and wolves in Slovenia and Croatia and on khulan and other large herbivores in the southeast Gobi.

The authors point out that they had difficulty finding information on border fences in these regions, especially details on exact location, length and construction of the fencing. "Unfortunately, a systematic overview of these details is lacking, making it impossible to conduct any form of spatially explicit analysis of the real fragmentation effect of these structures," they write. "There are likely to be very different effects of structures on different species, migratory large herbivores and large carnivores being most affected."

Another main takeaway: The researchers estimated there is a total of 30,000 kilometers of border fencing in the study area and that Central Asia is one of the most heavily fenced regions on the planet.

The authors stress the need for scientists and policymakers to work together. "The opportunities for transboundary cooperation in wildlife conservation are shrinking in many regions," they write. "When examining the geopolitical situation and the very real security challenges that some countries in Eurasia are facing at the moment, it seems likely that many of these fences are here to stay and that more are likely to appear, while existing fences are strengthened. This means that conservationists will have to recognise the potential impacts of these fences and adapt population management accordingly."

Other Resources for Journalists

- U.S. Customs and Border Protection provides background information on its border security efforts, including the historical evolution of its strategies.
- Some of the scholars with expertise in border barriers include: Reece Jones, an associate professor of geography at

the University of Hawaii at Manoa; Elisabeth Vallet, director of the Center for Geopolitical Studies at the University of Quebec-Montreal; Jeremy Slack, an assistant professor of geography at the University of Texas, El Paso who runs the Immigration and Border Communities-Research Experience for Undergraduates; Kenneth Madsen, an associate professor of geography at Ohio State University; and Peter Andreas, a professor of international studies and political science at Brown University.

- Staff members of the Arizona Republic and USA Today Network won the 2018 Pulitzer Prize in explanatory reporting for their coverage of Trump's pledge to construct a wall along the U.S.-Mexico border.

Periodical and Internet Sources Bibliography

The following articles have been selected to supplement the diverse views presented in this chapter.

Associated Press, "Separation of Parents, Kids at U.S.-Mexico Border: How the Trump Administration Got Here." CBC, June 18, 2018. www.cbc.ca/news/world/border-children-parents-separation-trump-1.4710055.

Aisha Dodwell, "7 Reasons Why We Should Have Open Borders." New Internationalist, November 29, 2017. newint.org/blog/2017/11/29/why-open-borders.

"Fact Sheet: Family Separation at the U.S.-Mexico Border", National Immigration Forum, June 20, 2018. https://immigrationforum.org/article/factsheet-family-separation-at-the-u-s-mexico-border/.

Robert Farley, "Is Mexico Paying for the Wall Through USMCA?" FactCheck.org, December 14, 2018. www.factcheck.org/2018/12/is-mexico-paying-for-the-wall-through-usmca/.

Jeffrey Miron, "Forget the Wall Already, It's Time for the U.S. to Have Open Borders." *USA Today*, July 31, 2018. www.usatoday.com/story/opinion/2018/07/31/open-borders-help-economy-combat-illegal-immigration-column/862185002/.

Mark Niquette, "Trump Said Mexico Would Pay for the Border Wall. Now What?" Bloomberg Quint, May 24, 2019. www.bloombergquint.com/quicktakes/about-that-wall-trump-said-mexico-would-be-paying-for-quicktake.

Jeremy A. Schwartz, "Tech Could Supplement a Physical Border Wall, But Many Questions Remain." Government Technology, February 22, 2018. www.govtech.com/public-safety/Tech-Could-Supplement-a-Physical-Border-Wall-But-Many-Questions-Remain.html.

Alex Ward, "The US Is Sending 5,000 Troops to the Border. Here's What They Can and Can't Do." VOX, October 31, 2018. www.vox.com/2018/10/29/18026646/military-border-caravan-immigrants-trump-caravan.

CHAPTER 2

Should Special Rules Apply to Refugee Immigrants?

Chapter Preface

T he United States has long been known to recognize the plight of refugees escaping war and other types of persecution. However, recent federal policies and actions have been allegedly unlawful. Witnesses and human rights activists attest to illegal means used to keep refugees in endangered situations. Whether special rules should apply to refugee immigrants lies at the core of debates between governments and humanitarian activists. Even when a law is relaxed, skeptics believe the relief will only be temporary. Still, immigrants have rejoiced when Temporary Protected Status has been eliminated, because family members could then stay together a while longer in the United States. At particular risk are the children in these families who were born in the United States. They face losing an undocumented parent to deportation to the home country.

Part of the issue stems from the geographic point of entry. Refugees may not be fully cognizant of official ports of entry to the United States. But, some viewpoints present evidence that even when refugees seeking asylum approach an official entry port, they are turned away unlawfully. They then have few alternatives and an illegal entry becomes a choiceless choice.

Nine cities and the State of California have taken a stand against the Trump administration. Municipal and state leaders have enacted a variety of strategies to protect the rights and to defend immigrants. These cities, called sanctuary cities, including Los Angeles, Chicago, and New York City, have large immigrant populations. Local government is willing to dedicate city funds to help these populations even if that means a face-off against the federal government or elimination of federal funds for their cities.

The following chapter presents opposing viewpoints concerning special refugee status and whether refugees from unstable, war-torn countries should be allowed into the United States at or between US ports of entry.

> *"Those with U.S.-citizen children will be confronted with the dilemma of either bringing their children with them, giving up their children's lives in the United States (for many, the only lives they know), or being separated from their children."*

Temporary Protected Status for Refugees Is in Danger

Dara Lind

In the following viewpoint, Dara Lind argues that while a federal court in California judged against the Trump administration's move to end refugee Temporary Protected Status, it may just be temporary relief. Still, immigrant families are hopeful that they may remain in the United States without the threat of breaking their families apart. At risk in particular are the children born to these immigrants of El Salvador, Haiti, Nicaragua, and Sudan in the United States. Dara Lind is senior reporter at Vox, writing about immigration issues. She is based in the Washington, DC, area.

"Judge Blocks Trump's Efforts to End Temporary Protected Status for 300,000 Immigrants," by Dara Lind, Vox Media, October 4, 2018. Reprinted by permission.

As you read, consider the following questions:

1. What does Temporary Protected Status mean?
2. How did the federal government handle TPS cases before the Trump administration came into power?
3. What must the Supreme Court do to make this temporary relief more permanent?

The judicial resistance against the Trump administration's immigration policy continues.

On Wednesday night, a federal judge in California put a hold on the administration's plans to stop renewing the legal status of 300,000 people living in the US from El Salvador, Haiti, Nicaragua and Sudan.

All four countries were set to lose Temporary Protected Status over the next year—meaning that immigrants who'd lived in the US for years and often decades would be forced to leave or risk deportation. The more than 1,000 Sudanese living in the US with TPS, for example, were set to lose their legal status on November 2, 2018—less than a month from the ruling granting them a reprieve.

The ruling is a preliminary injunction—it holds the status quo in place until the courts have issued a final ruling in the case Ramos v. Nielsen, on whether the Trump administration violated the law in ending TPS for these countries. But in Wednesday's ruling, Judge Edward Chen of the Northern District of California indicated that he's likely to rule against the administration in his final analysis, too.

It's yet another judicial setback for an administration that has seen most of its signature immigration initiatives—the first and second versions of the travel ban, its attempts to defund "sanctuary cities," and its efforts to end the Deferred Action for Childhood Arrivals (DACA) program that protects about 700,000 unauthorized immigrants from deportation—halted by the courts.

More specifically, it's another nationwide injunction against the administration (a practice administration officials and conservative

Supreme Court justices are getting increasingly annoyed with) from a judge in the Ninth Circuit Court of Appeals (which Trump has painted as a rogue court).

At some point, it's likely that the TPS case will make its way to the Supreme Court, where the administration will likely prevail—if it has appointed a conservative justice by then. In the meantime, the TPS holders who were forced to make plans to leave the country or slink into the shadows after decades in the US now have some hope they'll be able to stay—but even less certainty about how long that will be.

Trump's U-turn on TPS Threatens to Uproot Hundreds of Thousands of Longtime US Residents

The federal government has the power to grant Temporary Protected Status (TPS) for residents of a certain country who are in the US when that country suffers from a disaster. The legal protection allows them to stay and work in the US legally when their home country wouldn't be safe to return to.

TPS can only be granted for six to 18 months at a time; the government is supposed to keep reviewing the conditions in a given country to see if it's recovered enough to send people back. But before Trump, the government generally kept renewing the designations—especially for countries that weren't in great shape generally. As a result, 250,000 Salvadorans have been living in the US on TPS since a 2001 earthquake; a few thousand Nicaraguans and Sudanese have had TPS in the US for even longer.

Under Trump, though, the administration's taken a hard line that "temporary means temporary"—and that if a country's current problems weren't obviously connected to the original disaster that spurred a TPS designation, it didn't deserve TPS anymore. Trump's DHS has ended TPS for seven out of nine countries it's reviewed.

To TPS holders themselves, this has been a tremendous shock creating ripples of anxiety. For activists (often also TPS holders), it's a sign that the Trump administration is letting Donald Trump's aversion to immigrants from "shithole countries" (a comment that he made in a discussion about TPS holders) drive its policymaking.

Internal government documents obtained in this lawsuit (and a similar lawsuit in Massachusetts) have certainly indicated that decisions on TPS were made from the top down. In one email exchange, top officials pushed career staffers to include more positive facts about life in Haiti, because a negative report about country conditions didn't gel with the decision to end TPS for it.

In another, then-acting Homeland Security Secretary Elaine Duke appears to have shortened the amount of time given to Nicaraguans before losing their TPS from 18 months to 12—after a last-minute phone call with then-White House Homeland Security Adviser Tom Bossert.

The Ruling Doesn't Say the Government Made the Wrong Decision to End TPS for These Countries— Just That It Went About It the Wrong Way

In theory, the decision to end TPS for a given country isn't subject to judicial review. But Judge Chen has ruled that the courts can say that the process by which DHS makes those decisions can be reviewed, and that it's supposed to conform to the Administrative Procedure Act (which sets out how the executive branch is supposed to make policy decisions).

Wednesday night's ruling is based in the harm that would be caused to TPS holders being forced to leave the US.

> TPS beneficiaries thus risk being uprooted from their homes, jobs, careers, and communities. They face removal to countries to which their children and family members may have little or no ties and which may not be safe. Those with U.S.-citizen children will be confronted with the dilemma of either bringing their children with them, giving up their children's lives in the United States (for many, the only lives they know), or being separated from their children.

Compared to that, the government couldn't maintain that it would be harmed if TPS holders from Sudan (who are supposed to leave by November 2, 2018) were allowed to stay a few extra months.

But a preliminary injunction also has to consider the odds that the government will ultimately lose the case—that the preliminary injunction will become permanent.

In Chen's view, the Trump administration's shift from looking at all conditions in a country when reviewing TPS, to looking only at whether the country was still feeling direct impacts of the original disaster, probably violated the APA's prohibition on making "silent" policy changes without public notice. (The government contends that it didn't change the policies around TPS, just the emphases given to various factors.)

The more inflammatory claim in the suit is that the decision to end TPS was grounded in Trump's own racial animus, and therefore unconstitutional. But this ruling didn't exactly endorse that idea—it just allows that there are "serious questions" that deserve further review.

That's enough for a preliminary injunction, given the harm to TPS holders. But it means this ruling (like the rulings against Trump's efforts to end DACA) doesn't point to a final ruling that forces the Trump administration to let TPS holders stay indefinitely. It's more likely to point to a final ruling that will force the administration to go through the decision-making process again, the "right way"—even if Trump officials find a way to get to the same result.

A Nine-Justice Supreme Court Will Probably Side with Trump

Judge Chen's injunction indicates he probably won't rule for the government. And it's fair to assume the Ninth Circuit will rule against the Trump administration on an immigration case. But the Supreme Court has already shown more deference to the administration on immigration policy than lower courts have, with the travel-ban cases, and it's fair to say that the conservative wing of the court will find it inappropriate to dissect the process behind a decision the administration is legally supposed to make.

That means Trump needs Brett Kavanaugh (or, in theory, another conservative justice) on the court, to give the conservative wing a 5-4 majority instead of creating a 4-4 stalemate that lets the Ninth Circuit's ruling stand.

Some reports have indicated that if Kavanaugh's nomination goes down and Democrats retake the Senate in the midterm elections, Trump will simply refuse to nominate an alternative, and allow the court to stay at eight justices for the foreseeable future. Rulings like this one show why this is such a terrible idea for Trump.

Without a five-justice majority, conservatives can't overturn Ninth Circuit rulings siding against the president's immigration policy. They can't even beat back the scope of a nationwide injunction, and stop judges like Chen from setting policy for the entire US. (Though in cases like the TPS case, it would be very hard to enforce an injunction where immigrants' legal status was determined by what state they were living in.)

Of course, Kavanaugh will probably be confirmed. Once that happens, the days of the judicial resistance will be numbered.

More Hope—but Also More Uncertainty

In the short term, Wednesday night's ruling is very good news for the 300,000 TPS holders affected by the ruling—and for the US-citizen children many of them have. The lead plaintiff in the case, 14-year-old Christa Ramos (whose parents are from El Salvador), issued a statement after the ruling: "Ever since the TPS terminations were announced, I have been wondering how I can live a normal life if I am about to lose my mom. Today, my family and I are celebrating."

It's especially good news for the 1,000 Sudanese TPS holders who had barely a month to stay in the US legally, who will almost certainly be able to stay past November 2 under this injunction. It's probably also good news for the 5,000 Nicaraguan TPS holders whose leave-by date was January 19, 2019. While Judge Chen's injunction says he'll issue a final ruling as quickly as possible, it may easily take more than three months. These people might ultimately have to leave the US, if Judge Chen (or a higher court) rules for the government, but they'll buy some time.

But unless the Supreme Court ultimately sides against the government—or the Trump administration gives up and stops fighting—this is just a temporary reprieve. It doesn't force the administration to formally renew TPS, much less grant any more permanent legal status. And it doesn't even require the administration to delay the departure timeline—in theory, if a ruling for the government came down on November 3, Sudanese TPS holders could be immediately eligible for deportation.

This means that instead of being forced to choose between leaving the US and becoming unauthorized, TPS holders will have to make two kinds of plans for their lives—a Plan A for what they'll do as they continue to be allowed to live in the US legally, and a Plan B for what will happen if that reprieve ends.

"There have been families turned away nine times when they do walk up to a point of entry and say that they are seeking asylum."

Illegal Immigrant Refugees Will No Longer Be Able to Seek Asylum

NPR

In the following viewpoint, National Public Radio (NPR) host Scott Simon interviews Lindsay Harris of the American Immigration Lawyers Association about the Trump administration's denial of asylum to illegal immigrants. Together they point up the obstacles now put in place that force asylum-seekers into a kind of no-man's land. This new rule would supercede the 1980 law that allows those seeking asylum safe haven irrespective of how they arrived in America. Harris also discusses how refugees are unlawfully being turned away from legal ports of entry. Scott Simon is a journalist and broadcaster. He hosts the Weekend Edition *news show on NPR.*

As you read, consider the following questions:

1. What is the credible fear interview?
2. What is the reasonable fear interview?
3. What reasons does this viewpoint give for immigrants not entering at an official US port of entry?

Scott Simon speaks with Lindsay Harris of the American Immigration Lawyers Association about the Trump administration's new rule to deny migrants who enter the U.S. illegally from seeking asylum.

SCOTT SIMON, HOST: The American Civil Liberties Union, Southern Poverty Law Center and other immigrant rights groups have filed lawsuits against the Trump administration's new proclamation that would deny asylum to people who enter the country illegally. The president signed that order yesterday before flying to France. We're joined now by Lindsay Harris, vice chair of the National Asylum and Refugee Committee at the American Immigration Lawyers Association. Thanks very much for being with us.

LINDSAY HARRIS: Thank you so much for having me.

SIMON: I don't know what a difference between an executive order and a proclamation is.

HARRIS: Well, proclamations seem to be more rare. They do kind of echo of something royal, but it has basically the same effect as an executive order.

SIMON: And how would this change what somebody who wants to apply for asylum must do?

HARRIS: Well, it's trying to bar asylum for people who enter the U.S. in between ports of entry.

SIMON: When you say...

HARRIS: So those people are...

SIMON: When you say—forgive me. When you say in between ports of entry, would some people phrase that as illegally?

HARRIS: Yes. The administration calls that illegal entry.

SIMON: You don't call it illegal entry if it's not through a port of entry.

HARRIS: I don't. I don't call it illegal entry when somebody is seeking asylum because our asylum laws have recognized since 1980 the right for any person who is present in the U.S. regardless of how they got here to seek asylum.

SIMON: And it provides for them to be able to apply for asylum within their first year, as I recall reading the law.

HARRIS: Right. That's another bar that was put in place in 1996, that you're supposed to file within one year of arrival. So what the administration has done this week is try to create a new bar. But that bar actually does conflict directly with the statute, with the Refugee Act from 1980.

SIMON: Ms. Harris, what do you say to those Americans who might say, look; I have a world of sympathy for people who want asylum, it's important for America to be that beacon in the world, but come through a port of entry and apply, don't slip in over the border?

HARRIS: Well, there's a number of reasons why it's very difficult and sometimes impossible for people to come through ports of entry. Often, they don't know they're supposed to do that. People are fleeing for their lives and don't actually know what the proper procedure is or even what asylum is. They just know they're trying to get to a safe place. Others also - what we've been seeing, especially in the last couple of years, is people being unlawfully turned away from ports of entry. Even yesterday, there were reports of the bridge, you know, between El Paso and Ciudad Juarez being closed down. And there's also—so people are waiting for days, sometimes even months, at the border. There have been families turned away nine times when they do walk up to a point of entry and say that they are seeking asylum. And many people don't have the resources to sit and wait in Mexico. And furthermore, there is targeting of migrants and asylum-seekers in Mexico that makes it unsafe for them to stay there. So there's lots of reasons why people would instead cross the river, come over the border and then turn themselves in immediately to Customs and Border Protection.

SIMON: What does the law say as to what the government— what authorities need to do when someone says, I'm here to apply for asylum?

HARRIS: So the law says that, basically, you're then supposed to be asked four questions. And the questions are along the lines of, do you have a fear of returning to your home country? Are you here to seek asylum? Would you be tortured if you returned? If somebody says yes in response to any of those questions, it's supposed to be an automatic referral to a credible fear interview, which is kind of a threshold test to determine whether someone could be eligible for asylum. What Trump and the administration have done in the last couple days is try and take away that credibility fear interview for people who cross in between ports of entry.

SIMON: And if there's no interview, there is no way of gauging their appeal for asylum.

HARRIS: Well, yeah. Well, actually, the government does provide another type of interview that they've made clear they're not taking away, which is called reasonable fear. But then people will only be eligible for a much lesser form of protection called withholding of removal rather than asylum. So they're still going to very likely go through the process and have the full adjudication in immigration court. So nothing about this is actually going to save the government any time, energy or resources.

SIMON: Lindsay Harris, professor of law, co-director of the immigration clinic at the District of Columbia School of Law, thanks so much for being with us.

HARRIS: Thank you very much.

> "*On Trump's vow to withhold federal
> funding from 'sanctuary cities,'
> [Chicago mayor Rahm] Emanuel
> said, 'The United States government
> cannot coerce the city, cannot
> blackmail the city, cannot punish the
> city into changing its value system.'*"

Sanctuary Cities Are Helping Immigrants Outwit ICE

John Carlos Frey

In the following viewpoint, John Carlos Frey argues that several so-called "sanctuary cities" across the country and the state of California are working to help immigrants buck the system and protecting them against Immigration and Customs Enforcement (ICE), whom he terms "Trump's dragnet." A wide range of actions include passing municipal laws to help immigrants avoid deportation for petty offenses in Denver, training personnel how to handle immigration agents in Portland, using millions of city dollars to help immigrants in New York City and Chicago, and suing the federal government in Los Angeles. John Carlos Frey is an Emmy Award–winning freelance investigative journalist and documentarian.

"How 'Sanctuary Cities' Are Helping Immigrants Outwit ICE," by John Carlos Frey, The Marshall Project, June 20, 2017. Reprinted by permission.

As you read, consider the following questions:

1. According to this viewpoint, which cities are called sanctuary cities? Why are they called this?
2. What actions is the state of California taking?
3. What type of violations put illegal immigrants on ICE notice?

Within days of taking office, President Donald Trump signed an executive order threatening to stop aid to communities that don't fully cooperate with federal officials to help deport immigrants. Many mayors of these so-called sanctuary cities were outraged and vowed to continue resisting Trump's immigration agenda.

Although a federal judge blocked Trump's plan, these localities still face possible loss of some federal funds as well as reprisals from conservative legislators. Now the conflict between Trump and the mayors has escalated from a war of words to a war of tactics as some "sanctuary cities"—and one state—are taking action to help immigrants avoid Trump's dragnet. Here are several examples:

Denver

In May, the city passed municipal sentencing reform that could help immigrants avoid deportation for petty offenses. Federal rules put immigrants on Immigration and Customs Enforcement radar when they are convicted of certain types of crimes that carry a sentence of at least a year. Prior to Denver's reform measure, all criminal violations of city ordinance carried the same penalty—up to 365 days. The new sentencing guidelines place the penalty for low-level violations under 364 days, which could help keep some immigrants off the federal books. "Denver is committed to taking actions that will protect our people's rights and keep our city safe, welcoming and open," Mayor Michael Hancock said in a statement after signing the law.

Los Angeles

Los Angeles has an estimated 1.5 million undocumented immigrants, the most in any U.S. city. And the Los Angeles Police Department has a 40-year history of not enforcing immigration law, dating back to former Republican Gov. Pete Wilson's crackdown on the undocumented. It doesn't appear that Trump's aggressive deportation strategy is changing L.A.'s stance. Mayor Eric Garcetti has declared he will sue the federal government for any withholding of funds or pressure placed on the L.A.P.D. to enforce immigration laws. He also set up a $10 million legal defense fund for people threatened with deportation. "This is a city that not only provides sanctuary," Garcetti said at a recent press conference. "We are a place that will go further and defend our immigrants."

California

The state Senate passed a bill in late March that officially would make California a sanctuary state. A defiant response to Trump's threat to defund "sanctuary cities," the legislation bars state and local law enforcement from using resources to help with immigration enforcement and prohibits law enforcement statewide from asking for immigration status. Connecticut, Colorado, New Mexico and Rhode Island already have similar statewide protections for undocumented immigrants, but this measure, expected to be signed by the governor, is the most far-reaching.

Santa Fe, N.M.

In late February 2017, the Santa Fe City Council passed a resolution reaffirming the city's status as a welcoming community for immigrants and refugees and adopting several new policies. Among the changes: City employees are now prohibited from disclosing sensitive information, including immigration status, about any person except as required by law. Also, city employees have been directed to refuse access to non-public areas of city property by federal immigration agents who don't have a warrant. Councilor

Sanctuary Cities Stand Their Ground to Protect Illegal Immigrants

PRESS RELEASE FOR IMMEDIATE DISTRIBUTION JANUARY 25, 2017 SANCTUARY CITIES MUST STAND THEIR GROUND AND PROTECT IMMIGRANTS ORANGE COUNTY

We condemn President Trump's executive orders signed today that represent hostility towards our immigrant communities and allow law enforcement agencies to engage in racial profiling. The actions taken today by this administration will start the construction of a wall in the U.S. southern border with Mexico, increase the number of border patrol agents, the revival of 287(g) agreements to allow local law enforcement agents to act as immigration officials and to threaten to cut federal funding to "Sanctuary Cities". This is a test to "Sanctuary Cities", specially those that have meaningful protections that go beyond symbolic rhetoric, to stand their ground and lead the resistance against an administration that is openly hostile towards our communities and capitalizes on the false narrative that immigrants are criminals. Cities must protect the due process, civil rights and human rights of its residents. They must use every single tool available to slow down, stall and challenge these draconian efforts by President Trump's administration. Fear and anxiety is growing in our communities as the anti-immigrant and nativist rhetoric continue to be validated by this administration. Vigilante and white supremacists groups will feel emboldened more than ever to harass and engage in violence against vulnerable populations. Resilience Orange County remains committed to organize and push back against the criminalization of our immigrant communities and any deportation efforts by this administration. #ICEOutofCa #Not1More

"Sanctuary Cities Must Stand Their Ground and Protect Immigrants," by Oswaldo Farias, Resilience Orange County.

Joseph Maestas said the measure was a way of "thumbing our nose at" the Trump administration.

Portland, Ore.

In May, in a partially symbolic move, the city council declared Portland a "sanctuary city," boldly stating its unwillingness to help ICE find and deport immigrants. The city is also providing resources to train staff on how to respond to federal immigration officials who request information on city employees or Portland residents. "The City of Portland will remain a welcoming, safe place for all people," Mayor Ted Wheeler wrote in a newspaper column.

Washington, D.C.

In response to the Trump administration's threat to withhold federal funding, Mayor Muriel Bowser said the District would continue to limit cooperation with deportation orders. "I will not let the residents of D.C. live in fear," she said. The City Council also unanimously passed a resolution vowing to maintain "sanctuary city" status. Meanwhile, Attorney General of the District of Columbia Karl Racine, an immigrant who fled political oppression in Haiti, said his office would protect the rights of all District residents, including undocumented immigrants.

Chicago

Like several other big city mayors, Mayor Rahm Emanuel has declared that Chicago will remain a safe haven for undocumented immigrants. In December, even before Trump took office, he pledged $1 million of city funds to assist immigrant families. On Trump's vow to withhold federal funding from "sanctuary cities," Emanuel said, "The United States government cannot coerce the city, cannot blackmail the city, cannot punish the city into changing its value system."

Milwaukee

In early February, the Milwaukee County Board of Supervisors declared the jurisdiction a sanctuary for immigrants and assured that no county money would be used to enforce federal immigration laws. "Some of the values and ideals that have been attacked by President Trump, we've now stood up against, and we've gone on record," said County Supervisor Marina Dimitrijevic.

New York City

In late January, Mayor Bill de Blasio announced he was socking away an additional $250 million a year in reserves for four years because of a "huge amount of uncertainty" stemming from Trump's threat to cut federal funds to "sanctuary cities" like New York, which is home to an estimated undocumented population of over 750,000. "The stroke of a pen in Washington does not change the people of New York City or our values," de Blasio said.

Boston

In January, Mayor Martin Walsh vowed he would physically protect and harbor undocumented immigrants if necessary. "I will use all of my power within lawful means to protect all Boston residents— even if that means using City Hall itself as a last resort," he said. "If you don't agree with me, there's an election in November."

> "When I was imprisoned in Syria for three years, I knew I was guilty for going against the government—but in Turkey I was imprisoned for no reason."

Turkey Unlawfully Deports Syrian War Refugees

Shawn Carrié and Asmaa Al Omar

In the following viewpoint, Shawn Carrié and Asmaa Al Omar argue that undocumented Syrian refugees in Turkey face arrest, detention and deportation back into the war zone they were trying to flee. The authors claim the methods used in Turkey are unlawful. Refugees seeing few options sign documents that place them right back where they started. Shawn Carrié is an Istanbul-based freelance reporter who covers conflict, migration, and culture in the Middle East. Asmaa Omar is also a freelance journalist writing about conflict and politics in the Middle East. She is based in Turkey.

As you read, consider the following questions:

1. What is Branch 500?
2. What is refoulement?
3. Does having proper documents protect Syrian refugees in Turkey?

"'It's Against the Law': Syrian Refugees Deported from Turkey Back to War," "by Shawn Carrié and Asmaa Al Omar, Guardian News and Media Limited, October 16, 2018. Reprinted by permission.

Tareq* can recall in detail each of the 22 times he climbed over the concrete border wall, dodged a flurry of bullets, and sprinted as fast as he could—until Turkish border guards caught him and turned him back.

On his 23rd attempt, the soldiers drove the 26-year-old Syrian to a police station called Branch 500 in Hatay. There they presented him with a choice: either stay in prison—for how long, they wouldn't say—or sign a paper and walk free.

"It's not like they're physically putting a gun to your head, but you have no other option," Tareq says. He signed and the next day he was driven across the border and dropped back where he had started, in Idlib.

It was only when he yet again crossed from Syria into Turkey that he understood the paper's significance. The Turkish authorities told him what he had signed at Branch 500 waived his claim for asylum protection.

As uncertainty hangs over Syria's final rebel-controlled enclave, where government and rebel forces are currently in a tense standoff, a Guardian investigation has found that undocumented Syrian refugees in Turkey face arrest, detention and deportation back to the war they fled. Some claim to have been coerced into signing statements saying they were returning of their own free will.

Human rights groups say this is in violation of international law, which prohibits refoulement—sending refugees back to war zones.

"These are clear-cut unlawful deportations because they are refugees—and sending them back amounts to refoulement," says Gerry Simpson, of Human Rights Watch in Geneva.

Turkey currently hosts more than 3.5 million Syrians—the highest number of refugees in the world—and has long boasted of an "open-door policy" towards Syrians. Now, as Russian and Syrian government forces close in on Idlib province, those trying to escape what is expected to be a bloodbath have found the doors to Turkey closing.

"We will not take responsibility for a wave of migration that may follow attacks in Idlib," interior minister Süleyman Soylu told reporters in September.

The refugee issue is hotly debated both domestically and amid tense relations with the EU, which gives billions of euros in aid to Turkey for its refugee population. President Tayyip Erdoğan supports hosting Syrians, while opposition parties call for sending them home.

But Turkish police have stepped up checkpoints and raids, arresting Syrians without documents or permits to travel outside the cities where they registered. Provincial authorities have effectively halted registrations for new arrivals, leaving them unable to work legally or even visit a hospital, and vulnerable to arrest.

After having been deported to Syria once already, Ashraf* is now in Istanbul, where he is working as a black market labourer and living with the constant fear of arrest. "I told the officer, 'Please don't send me to Idlib. I don't know anyone there. At least send me to my city, to Daraa,'" says Ashraf.

Shown a "voluntary return form" used by authorities in Branch 500, Ashraf says he recognises it as the same one the police had made him sign before deporting him to Idlib.

Even those with proper documents can be caught up in the system. Samer Tlass, 42, a lawyer from Homs, worked legally at a Syrian NGO in Gaziantep until June 2017, when he was caught in a police raid and taken to Oğuzeli removal centre.

Tlass said authorities at Oğuzeli told Syrians that if they signed voluntary returns, they could leave for Syria the next morning. Tlass refused. After 45 days, he was handed a deportation order for "working without a permit".

"It's ironic, I even used to give training on this to Syrians, about the law, and their rights," Tlass says. "What they are doing is against the law."

In a letter to the Guardian, Turkey's migration directorate denied that any deportations were carried out, stating that no Syrians are denied the chance to register or face arrest if they fail to do so.

"According to the prohibition of refoulement, Syrians in our country are not deported in any way," the letter says.

The Guardian spoke to several Syrians who described the Oğuzeli removal centre in detail. Prison-like, it was converted from a school into a detention facility with EU funding. It now houses 750 people, with detainees held six to a cell. Conditions have been the subject of lawsuits that reached Turkey's constitutional court. Sources detained there described how buses regularly came and went moving groups of 20-30 people in from other cities and out towards the nearby border.

Turkey typically detains foreigners slated for deportation in one of 19 provincial removal centres managed by the interior ministry. Turkey grants blanket protection to Syrians, even if they have entered the country illegally. Migration officials said that "under no circumstances" are Syrians held in centres. However, the ministry's own 2017 figures say that more than 50,000 Syrians were apprehended as "illegal migrants".

Detainees are entitled to legal aid but lawyers working on Syrian cases say that since they are in administrative detention, they can do little except appeal to move the case to an open court—by which time their clients are often gone.

"In many cases, detainees can't afford the lawyer's fees, so they just give up and sign the voluntary return form," says Samer Deyaei, one of a group of Syrian lawyers campaigning for the Oğuzeli detainees.

A UNHCR spokeswoman, Selin Ünal, says that so far this year the UN agency knows of more than 100 detainees at Oğuzeli who were scheduled for deportation to Syria.

"117 is the number of people we are aware of—who reached us," says Ünal. "There could be any number—we have no idea because we don't have regular access to these removal centres."

Each voluntary return form has space for three signatures—one for the person returning, one for authorities, and one for UN staff, the only international observers of the process. UN staff say they try to ensure they are free from coercion, but are restricted.

Authorities claim that 250,000 Syrians have opted to return, and that Branch 500 is the sole facility where they are processed.

UNHCR admits that its staff have overseen only a fraction of those—11,193 in total—and handed over all asylum registrations to Turkish authorities earlier this month.

A spokesperson for Hatay's governor admits that undocumented Syrians have been deported after being caught crossing the border "or in cases of crime", declining to elaborate further.

In October 2016 Turkey amended its temporary protection law to permit deportations in instances where an administrative court deems someone a threat to public order, security or health; or a terror suspect.

"Turkish people commit crimes and they face due process—Syrians commit crimes as well, and for some of them this due process requires them to be deported," says Harun Armagan, MP for the ruling Justice and Development Party (AKP) . "The number of people being deported is very low."

Deyaei said Turkish authorities should close legal loopholes that result in people being sent back into a war zone."

"Of course, Turkey has laws that stipulate what to do with criminals and terrorists," Deyaei says, "but I'm talking about people who maybe were in the wrong place, wrong time, or have some problem with papers and end up faced with two options: either sign the form or stay in prison—of course this is alarming."

Turkish courts have sometimes intervened when there is a risk of refoulement, but once the migration directorate issues a deportation order, it is final, Deyaei says. But for Samer Tlass, the only way out was with a visa to France, which he was only lucky enough to get because he had connections with civil society groups abroad.

"When I was imprisoned in Syria for three years, I knew I was guilty for going against the government—but in Turkey I was imprisoned for no reason," says Tlass. "This is an injustice."

*Names have been changed to protect identities

> "Instead of militarizing the border and peddling fear and discrimination, President Trump's administration should show compassion for those forced to flee their homes and must receive their requests for asylum without delay."

The US Government Unlawfully Stops Asylum Seekers

Erika Guevara Rosas

In the following viewpoint, Erika Guevara Rosas argues that research shows that US laws place thousands of asylum seekers in dire straits. These refugees face deportation and harm. Rosas claims the Trump administration violates both US and international law by not granting asylum and by insisting on using military forces to patrol the border between the United States and Mexico. She calls attention to a waitlist of asylum seekers that is manipulated by both Mexico and the United States. Erika Guevara Rosas is Americas director at Amnesty International, an organization advocating for human rights.

"Americas: US Government Endangers Asylum Seekers with Unlawful Policies," by Erika Guevara Rosas, Amnesty International, November 26, 2018. Reprinted by permission.

As you read, consider the following questions:

1. How many recommendations has Amnesty International made to American and Mexican governments in the name of humanitarian rights?
2. Name some of the issues associated with temporary shelters.
3. According to this viewpoint, what steps should Congress take?

Unlawful US border policies are leaving thousands of asylum seekers stranded in Mexico, where they are facing threats of deportation to their countries of origin, where they potentially face serious harm, Amnesty International said today following a research mission last week. Conditions could only worsen under a reported deal between both countries that, if agreed, would force asylum-seekers to remain in Mexico while their claims are processed, rather than allow them to enter the United States.

As a result of Amnesty International's research focusing on the treatment of refugees and migrants in the caravans in Guatemala, the southern Mexican state of Chiapas, Mexico City and Tijuana throughout October and November, the organization has today issued 26 recommendations to the US and Mexican governments, as well as to the authorities in Central American countries of origin and transit, to ensure human rights protections and humanitarian support for all those seeking asylum and en route, including calling on authorities to respect international standards on the use of force.

"Instead of militarizing the border and peddling fear and discrimination, President Trump's administration should show compassion for those forced to flee their homes and must receive their requests for asylum without delay, as required by US and international law," said Erika Guevara Rosas, Americas director at Amnesty International.

"For their part, the governments of Mexico and Central America must take urgent action to guarantee the safety and wellbeing of all these people on the move and ensure they do not suffer further human rights violations. If Mexico agrees to do the US government's dirty work at the expense of the caravan members' dignity and human rights, it is effectively paying for Trump's shameful border wall."

"The danger posed to desperate families patiently waiting their turn for asylum at the border is an emergency of the US government's own making," said Margaret Huang, executive director of Amnesty International USA.

"Using teargas in a situation where families, children and their parents were present was not only horrific, it was also a new low for this administration in its contempt for our shared human dignity and human rights."

Unsanitary Conditions and Unlawful Asylum Waitlists

On 18 November, Amnesty International visited Tijuana's Benito Juarez sports complex, a temporary shelter where the municipal government had accommodated approximately 3,000 migrants and asylum seekers who had arrived in the first of several caravans totaling 8,000 to 10,000 people across Mexico. They joined thousands of other people that US authorities have forced to wait in Tijuana for weeks or months before allowing them to request asylum at the border. On 22 November, US Secretary of State Pompeo declared that the US government plans to unlawfully deny people that right by refusing entry of the caravans into the United States.

Mexican federal, state and municipal officials separately confirmed to Amnesty International that the temporary shelter did not have sufficient food, water and health services, and that respiratory illnesses were spreading among those staying there.

Since at least April 2018, US and Mexican authorities have unlawfully required asylum seekers to put their names on a quasi-official asylum waitlist on the Tijuana side of the San Ysidro Port of Entry, instead of allowing people to request asylum directly at the border. The list is jointly coordinated by the asylum seekers themselves and Mexican authorities, in response to US limits on the number of asylum seekers they will receive each day. People seeking asylum without identity documents are prohibited from joining the list of those waiting to request asylum, and if they miss the day their number is called, they risk losing their places entirely.

By turning away asylum-seekers at ports of entry, US authorities are violating their right to seek asylum from persecution and manufacturing an emergency along the border. This queue along the border exposes people who seek asylum to risks of detention and deportation by Mexican immigration officials, and exploitation by criminal gangs.

On 21 November, Amnesty International reviewed the list, which contained the names of around 4,320 people, including about 2,000 caravan members, mostly from Honduras, who had arrived since 15 November. Those already on the list prior to the caravan's arrival had been waiting, on average, about five weeks in Tijuana before US authorities started processing their asylum claims. Officials from Mexico's National Institute of Migration (INM) and a Tijuana municipal official told Amnesty International that Mexican nationals comprised approximately 80 percent of those seeking asylum before the caravan arrived.

Mexican authorities cannot lawfully prevent people from exiting the country and seeking asylum at the US border. Yet Amnesty International confirmed with multiple sources in the Mexican government that Mexican immigration officials routinely take possession of the waitlist each night, and coordinate with US border authorities on how many asylum seekers from the list will be received each day. Amnesty International has received reports from Mexican officials speaking anonymously that raise doubts as to the supposed lack of capacity by US authorities to receive more people and indicate the pressure that the US government exercises on Mexican authorities to restrict entry of asylum seekers.

Mexican officials and asylum seekers at the San Ysidro Port of Entry told Amnesty International that US Customs and Border

Protection (CBP) officials there were recently accepting 30 to 70 asylum applications per day. On 16 November, CBP's San Ysidro Port Director told the Washington Post his staff could process 90 to 100 asylum seekers per day, provided that US Immigrations and Customs Enforcement (ICE) took custody within 72 hours of those asylum seekers whom they processed.

In a meeting with Amnesty International on 20 November, ICE officials declined to answer whether they were taking custody of asylum seekers in a timely fashion or faced any capacity constraints due to the recent arrival of the caravans, before abruptly ending the meeting.

Amnesty International calls on the US authorities to immediately respect people's right to claim asylum both at and between official ports of entry. Following the US government's declarations that they plan to unlawfully deny people in the caravans that right, Congress should decline to fund CBP operations absent rigorous congressional oversight of those operations and a written commitment from CBP to halt the illegal pushbacks of asylum-seekers both at and between US ports of entry. Amnesty International documented these pushbacks in a recent report.

People Seeking Asylum Face Risk of Deportation by Mexican Authorities

On 19 November, Tijuana's municipal police force announced that it had detained 34 caravan members for "public disorder" (including drinking beer on the street) and transferred them to INM for potential deportation. Amnesty International immediately asked INM to facilitate its access to interview the detainees, after receiving unverified reports that Tijuana's municipal police may have racially profiled, entrapped and/or extorted some of them, and that their detentions may have resulted in their separation from family members staying at the Benito Juarez sports facility. INM did not allow the organization to visit them.

On 20 November, a migrant rights expert with Mexico's National Human Rights Commission (CNDH) confirmed to Amnesty

International that one or more families had been separated by the detentions, but said CNDH had not yet interviewed any of the detainees to assess the validity of the charges against them. He noted that people who were part of the caravans were at high risk of deportation if detained by municipal police, since most either lack legal status in Mexico or their legal stay is due to expire soon, including those planning to seek asylum at the US border. Under Mexican migration law, municipal police are not allowed to carry out migratory revisions of people's documents—a task reserved for the INM.

Local media in Tijuana reported on 20 November that 40 caravan members had been detained by municipal police and then deported by INM. This detention is part of a wider trend in recent days, with the INM carrying out several mass detentions across Mexico in response to the caravan, including of families and children. In some cases, the number of people detained has reached the hundreds. On 25 November, Mexican authorities said that some of those who tried to cross into the United States and were met with teargas would be deported. Deporting people to countries were their lives are at risk, without giving them the chance to seek asylum, would violate Mexican and international law.

"Mexican municipal, state and federal authorities have struggled to accommodate and provide adequate humanitarian assistance for those stuck in Tijuana, and in some cases sought for Mexican immigration officials to deport people who are part of the caravans, potentially contrary to international law," said Erika Guevara Rosas.

"Mexico's National Migration Institute should urgently clarify whether all of those caravan members detained in recent days have been provided with opportunities to request asylum in Mexico or regularize their status and reunify with their children or other family members."

Amnesty International calls on the Mexican government to ensure and expedite proper screening of migrants and asylum seekers who may qualify for international protection; and provide provisional documentation to those awaiting reception at US ports of entry, to prevent them from being deported to their countries of origin while their cases are processed.

The organization also recommends authorities in countries of origin to address the factors that drive people to leave, while transit and receiving countries must ensure their health and safety, provide them with humanitarian assistance, respect their right to claim asylum, and prevent and investigate any abuses and human rights violations against them.

These recommendations are based on interviews that Amnesty International conducted with approximately 200 people travelling in the caravans—either individually or in groups, including several families, women travelling with children, and members of the LGTBI community—as well as information obtained from governments across the region, international organizations and civil society organizations present in the field.

> "*Winning asylum in the United States is no easy feat. Granted, the U.S. has recognized LGBT status as grounds for asylum since 1994, but the government keeps no records on how many claims it grants.*"

Ugandan LGBTQ Immigrants Seeking Asylum in the United States Will Face Further Obstacles

Richard Gonzales

In the following viewpoint, Richard Gonzales argues that LGBTQ immigrants spurred by a new Ugandan law criminalizing homosexuality will come to the United States seeking asylum, but they will face rough roads. Even finding advocates in Uganda to help LGBTQ individuals with the emigration process is a crime. In the United States, LGBTQ status has been accepted as grounds for asylum since 1994. However, US consulates do not easily grant asylum. Therefore, LGBTQ people looking to escape persecution come to America using different types of visas, if they are able. Richard Gonzales is NPR's National Desk Correspondent based in San Francisco, California.

As you read, consider the following questions:

1. According to this viewpoint, what countries have also declared homosexuality as a crime?
2. When did the United States start accepting immigrant LGBTQ status as grounds for asylum?
3. How many gay Ugandans were expected to seek asylum in the United States?

Even through a long-distance line from Uganda, you can hear the fear and anxiety in the young man's voice. Nathan, 19, is gay. NPR is not using his surname because he fears arrest.

"Right now we are not safe," he says. "Because we are hearing some people say ... 'If we get you, we will kill you. If we get you, we'll do something bad to you.' "

More than 70 countries have laws on the books criminalizing homosexuality, including Nigeria, Russia and India. And on Monday, Ugandan President Yoweri Museveni signed into law a measure that greatly expands the penalties for being gay in that country.

These laws also raise the likelihood of a tide of LGBT immigrants seeking asylum in the United States. But advocates say there is no smooth path for those claiming a fear of persecution.

In Uganda, the new law means a first-time offender can be sentenced to 14 years in prison. A lifetime sentence can be imposed for so-called "aggravated homosexuality," defined as sex with a minor or while HIV-positive.

Those sanctions are already driving gays and lesbians underground. Nathan and his partner fled Uganda's capital, Kampala, for a village where they hoped to find refuge. In the city, he says, he was threatened by neighbors for being gay.

"They take us as criminals. That's what I can say. They say we have evil in us," he says.

Even before Museveni signed the anti-gay bill, Ugandan activists were warning that the law would give license to more violence against gays.

Frank Mugisha, director of the group Sexual Minorities Uganda, says, "We're going to see people getting beaten on the streets, we're going to see people thrown out by their families, we're going to see people being evicted by their landlords, we're going to see people losing jobs, we're going to see people thrown out of school, because they are perceived or not as homosexuals. Even the suspicion will get someone in trouble."

And Mugisha has another prediction: "There's definitely going to be many people seeking asylum in different countries."

"A Lot of People Are In Panic Mode"

But winning asylum in the United States is no easy feat. Granted, the U.S. has recognized LGBT status as grounds for asylum since 1994, but the government keeps no records on how many claims it grants.

"It's an unconscionably hard process to seek asylum in the United States of America," says Melanie Nathan, a California-based lawyer who works on behalf of LGBT asylum seekers. She says it's virtually impossible for someone to knock on the door of a U.S. embassy abroad and ask for and receive asylum.

"So what happens is, they come to America on other types of visas. They come to America on workshop conference visas, on visitor's visas," she says. "And once they are here, people have a year to apply for asylum. The average person—especially younger people in Uganda, for example—will never get that initial visa and don't have money even to fly here."

Still, based on her social media contacts in Uganda, Nathan estimates anywhere between 2,000 and 3,000 gay Ugandans will seek asylum in the U.S. or other countries.

Nathan says she has what she calls her "Schindler's List"— "people that have been trying to escape." Since the signing of the new law in Uganda, "my phone has been going crazy, my messages have been crazy," she says. "A lot of people are in panic mode right now."

For its part, the Obama administration calls the new Ugandan law "more than an affront and a danger to the gay community" there. And in a statement, Secretary of State John Kerry has called for a repeal of the law.

"We are beginning an internal review with the Government of Uganda to ensure that all dimensions of our engagement, including assistance programs uphold our anti-discrimination policies and principles and reflect our values," the statement says.

But if the U.S. were to make it easier for Ugandans to get asylum, it's not likely to happen soon, if at all. That's what Nathan, the young man in Uganda, found out when a group of gay activists talked with U.S. Embassy officials there.

"They say they don't have asylum," he says. "So people, we have to fight for [our rights] ourselves."

But that's a difficult proposition in the East African country, where advocating for gay rights is also a criminal offense.

Periodical and Internet Sources Bibliography

The following articles have been selected to supplement the diverse views presented in this chapter.

Joshua Barajas, "What's Happening with Asylum-Seekers at the Border?" *PBS News Hour*, November 26, 2018. www.pbs.org/ newshour/nation/whats-happening-with-asylum-seekers-at-the-border.

Michael N. Barnett, "Is Trump's Refugee Policy Really So Extraordinary? The Walk Isn't, But the Talk Is," *Washington Post*, October 26, 2018. www.washingtonpost.com/news/ monkey-cage/wp/2018/10/26/is-trumps-refugee-policy-really-so-extraordinary-the-walk-isnt-but-the-talk-is/?utm_term=. efc2bf32ade2.

Astrid Galvan and Morgan Lee, "Trump Sanctuary City Idea Could Help Migrants Stay in US," Associated Press News, April 14, 2019. apnews.com/e991a0409f7c475ba48e827e232b6cfe.

International Rescue Committee, "Behind the Headlines: Temporary Protected Status," Rescue.org, October 4,2018. www.rescue.org/ article/behind-headlines-temporary-protected-status.

Gabrielle Levy, "Five Things to Know about Immigration and Asylum in the U.S.," *U.S. News & World Report*, June 25, 2018. www. usnews.com/news/national-news/articles/2018-06-25/five-things-to-know-about-immigration-and-asylum-in-the-us.

Gary McIndoe, "This Is What LGBTI+ People Have to Go through to Gain Asylum in the UK," *Independent*, July 29, 2018. www. independent.co.uk/voices/lgbt-rights-gay-lesbian-bisexual-transgender-asylum-uk-a8468456.html.

Jeffrey S. Passel and D'vera Cohen, "U.S. Unauthorized Immigrant Total Dips to Lowest Level in a Decade," Pew Research Center, November 27, 2018. www.pewhispanic.org/2018/11/27/u-s-unauthorized-immigrant-total-dips-to-lowest-level-in-a-decade/

Deirdre Shesgreen and Alan Gomez, "Sanctuary Cities for Illegal Immigrants? Here's What You Need to Know," *USA Today*, April 12, 2019. www.usatoday.com/story/news/world/2019/04/12/ sanctuary-cities-illegal-immigrants-can-carry-many-definitions/3449063002/.

OPPOSING
VIEWPOINTS®
SERIES

CHAPTER 3

Do Immigrants Weaken a Country?

Chapter Preface

In a 2014 speech, President Barack Obama announced changes to US immigration policy. In this speech he discussed an action plan of increased law enforcement along the border, a smoother process for highly-skilled workers and graduate students, and a pledge to deal responsibly with undocumented immigrants.

All that changed in January 2017 when President Donald Trump took office. Suddenly, the debate over whether immigrants strengthen or weaken the country seemed especially volatile. On the one hand, immigrants can take the place of retiring workers in the labor force. On the other hand, the president's new policies impeded the entry of highly-skilled professionals into the country.

Another debate issue is the connection between immigrants, both legal and illegal, and crime rates. Research has shown that when immigrants settle into neighborhoods that share their culture, crime rates are relatively low and register below the rate of native-born Americans. But when there are two or more cultures and those cultures clash, that situation can give rise to violence and other crimes. Yet, many political pundits insist the crime rate is higher because of immigrants. Learning English is another issue. Some Americans believe that all immigrants should be required to learn and use English in their own best interests. Not only would this give them a greater set of basic survival skills, but knowing America's common language will help them advocate for their own rights, connect them to the American community, and empower their children.

The following chapter explores issues connected with immigrants' value to a nation. It examines whether differences exist between documented and undocumented workers. These viewpoints also demonstrate the shift in policy caused by a new presidential administration and its effect on immigration process, crime rates, and the economy.

> *"Immigrants are also projected to drive future growth in the U.S. working-age population through at least 2035."*

Immigrants Will Replace Retiring Baby Boomers in the American Workforce

Gustavo López, Kristen Bialik, and Jynnah Radford

In the following viewpoint, Gustavo López, Kristen Bialik and Jynnah Radford argue that the United States is home to more immigrants than any other country. Nearly half of these settle in California, Texas, and New York. The majority of immigrants come from India, Mexico, China, and Cuba. Those from Asia are more likely to hold college degrees. As Baby Boomers head into retirement, immigrant workers are expected to pick up the slack. Gustavo López is a former research analyst at Pew Research in Washington, DC. Kristen Bialek and Jynnah Radford are research assistants at Pew Research.

"Key Findings About U.S. Immigrants," by Gustavo López, Kristen Bialik and Jynnah Radford, Pew Research Center, November 30, 2018.

As you read, consider the following questions:

1. What percentage of the American population are immigrants? How does that compare with 1970? 1890?
2. Which immigrant group has the lowest naturalization rate? Why?
3. What percentage of the American workforce are lawful immigrants?

The United States has more immigrants than any other country in the world. Today, more than 40 million people living in the U.S. were born in another country, accounting for about one-fifth of the world's migrants in 2016. The population of immigrants is also very diverse, with just about every country in the world represented among U.S. immigrants.

Pew Research Center regularly publishes statistical portraits of the nation's foreign-born population, which include historical trends since 1960. Based on these portraits, here are answers to some key questions about the U.S. immigrant population.

How Many People in the U.S. Are Immigrants?

The U.S. foreign-born population reached a record 43.7 million in 2016. Since 1965, when U.S. immigration laws replaced a national quota system, the number of immigrants living in the U.S. has more than quadrupled. Immigrants today account for 13.5% of the U.S. population, nearly triple the share (4.7%) in 1970. However, today's immigrant share remains below the record 14.8% share in 1890, when 9.2 million immigrants lived in the U.S.

What Is the Legal Status of Immigrants in the U.S.?

Most immigrants (76%) are in the country legally, while a quarter are unauthorized, according to new Pew Research Center estimates based on census data adjusted for undercount. In 2016, 45% were naturalized U.S. citizens.

Some 27% of immigrants were permanent residents and 5% were temporary residents in 2016. Another 24% of all immigrants were unauthorized immigrants. From 1990 to 2007, the unauthorized immigrant population tripled in size—from 3.5 million to a record high of 12.2 million. During the Great Recession, the number declined by 1 million and since then has leveled off. In 2016, there were 10.7 million unauthorized immigrants in the U.S., accounting for 3.3% of the nation's population.

The decline in the unauthorized immigrant population is due largely to a fall in the number from Mexico—the single largest group of unauthorized immigrants in the U.S. Between 2007 and 2016, this group decreased by more than 1 million. Meanwhile, there was a rise in the number from Central America.

Do All Lawful Immigrants Choose to Become U.S. Citizens?

Not all lawful permanent residents choose to pursue U.S. citizenship. Those who wish to do so may apply after meeting certain requirements, including having lived in the U.S. for five years. In fiscal year 2017, 986,851 immigrants applied for naturalization. The number of naturalization applications has climbed in recent years, though the annual totals remain below the 1.4 million applications filed in 2007.

Generally, most immigrants eligible for naturalization apply to become citizens. However, Mexican lawful immigrants have the lowest naturalization rate overall. Language and personal barriers, lack of interest and financial barriers are among the top reasons for choosing not to naturalize cited by Mexican-born green card holders, according to a 2015 Pew Research Center survey.

Where Do Immigrants Come From?

Mexico is the top origin country of the U.S. immigrant population. In 2016, 11.6 million immigrants living in the U.S. were from there, accounting for 26% of all U.S. immigrants. The next largest origin groups were those from China (6%), India (6%), the Philippines (4%) and El Salvador (3%).

By region of birth, immigrants from South and East Asia combined accounted for 27% of all immigrants, a share equal to that of Mexico. Other regions make up smaller shares: Europe/Canada (13%), the Caribbean (10%), Central America (8%), South America (7%), the Middle East (4%) and sub-Saharan Africa (4%).

Who Is Arriving Today?

More than 1 million immigrants arrive in the U.S. each year. In 2016, the top country of origin for new immigrants coming into the U.S. was India, with 126,000 people, followed by Mexico (124,000), China (121,000) and Cuba (41,000).

By race and ethnicity, more Asian immigrants than Hispanic immigrants have arrived in the U.S. each year since 2010. Immigration from Latin America slowed following the Great Recession, particularly from Mexico, which has seen net decreases in U.S. immigration over the past few years.

Asians are projected to become the largest immigrant group in the U.S. by 2055, surpassing Hispanics. Pew Research Center estimates indicate that in 2065, Asians will make up some 38% of all immigrants; Hispanics, 31%; whites, 20%; and blacks, 9%.

Is the Immigrant Population Growing?

New immigrant arrivals have fallen, mainly due to a decrease in the number of unauthorized immigrants coming to the U.S. The fall in the growth of the unauthorized immigrant population can partly be attributed to more Mexican immigrants leaving the U.S. than coming in.

Looking forward, immigrants and their descendants are projected to account for 88% U.S. population growth through 2065, assuming current immigration trends continue. In addition to new arrivals, U.S. births to immigrant parents will be important to future U.S. growth. In 2016, the percentage of women giving birth in the past year was higher among immigrants (7.4%) than to future U.S. growth. In 2016, the percentage of women giving birth in the past year was higher among immigrants (7.4%) than among the U.S. born (5.9%). While U.S.-born women gave birth to over 3 million children that year, immigrant women gave birth to more than 750,000.

How Many Immigrants Have Come to the U.S. As Refugees?

Since the creation of the federal Refugee Resettlement Program in 1980, about 3 million refugees have been resettled in the U.S – more than any other country.

In fiscal 2017, a total of 53,716 refugees were resettled in the U.S. The largest origin group of refugees was the Democratic Republic of the Congo, followed by Iraq, Syria, Somalia, and Burma (Myanmar). Among all refugees admitted in that fiscal year, 22,861 are Muslims (43%) and 25,194 are Christians (47%). California, Texas and New York resettled nearly a quarter of all refugees admitted in fiscal 2016.

Where Do Most U.S. Immigrants Live?

Roughly half (46%) of the nation's 43.7 million immigrants live in just three states: California (24%), Texas (11%) and New York (10%). California had the largest immigrant population of any state in 2016, at 10.7 million. Texas and New York had more than 4.5 million immigrants each.

In terms of regions, about two-thirds of immigrants lived in the West (34%) and South (33%). Roughly one-fifth lived in the Northeast (21%) and 11% were in the Midwest.

In 2016, most immigrants lived in just 20 major metropolitan areas, with the largest populations in New York, Los Angeles and Miami. These top 20 metro areas were home to 28.3 million immigrants, or 65% of the nation's total. Most of the nation's unauthorized immigrant population lived in these top metro areas as well.

How Do Immigrants Compare with the U.S. Population Overall in Education?

Immigrants in the U.S. as a whole have lower levels of education than the U.S.-born population. In 2016, immigrants were three times as likely as the U.S. born to have not completed high school (29% vs. 9%). However, immigrants were just as likely as the U.S. born to have a college degree or more, 32% and 30% respectively.

Educational attainment among U.S. immigrants in 2016Educational attainment varies among the nation's immigrant groups, particularly across immigrants from different regions of the world. Immigrants from Mexico (57%) and Central America (49%) are less likely to be high school graduates than the U.S. born (9%). On the other hand, immigrants from South and East Asia, Europe, Canada, the Middle East and sub-Saharan Africa were more likely than U.S.-born residents to have a bachelor's or advanced degree.

Among all immigrants, those from South and East Asia (52%) and the Middle East (47%) were the most likely to have a bachelor's degree or more. Immigrants from Mexico (6%) and Central America (9%) were the least likely to have a bachelor's or higher.

How Many Immigrants Are Working in the U.S.?

In 2016, about 28 million immigrants were working or looking for work in the U.S., making up some 17% of the total civilian labor force. Lawful immigrants made up the majority of the immigrant workforce, at 20.6 million. An additional 7.8 million immigrant workers are unauthorized immigrants, the first time since 2006 that the number was significantly below 8 million. They alone account for 4.8% of the civilian labor force, a dip from their peak of 5.4% in 2007. During the same period, the overall U.S. workforce grew, as did the number of U.S.-born workers and lawful immigrant workers.

Immigrants, regardless of legal status, work in a variety of jobs and do not make up the majority of workers in any U.S. industry. Lawful immigrants are most likely work in professional, management, or business and finance jobs (38%) or service jobs (21%). Unauthorized immigrants, by contrast, are most likely to be working in service (31%) or construction jobs (17%).

Immigrants are also projected to drive future growth in the U.S. working-age population through at least 2035. As the Baby Boom generation heads into retirement, immigrants and their children are expected to offset a decline in the working-age population by adding about 18 million people of working age between 2015 and 2035.

How Well Do Immigrants Speak English?

Among immigrants ages 5 and older, half (51%) are proficient English speakers—either speaking English very well (35%) or only speaking English at home (16%).

Immigrants from Mexico have the lowest rates of English proficiency (32%), followed by Central Americans (33%) and immigrants from South and East Asia (54%). Those from Europe or Canada (76%), sub-Saharan Africa (72%), and the Middle East (61%) have the highest rates of English proficiency.

The longer immigrants have lived in the U.S., the greater the likelihood they are English proficient. Some 44% of immigrants living in the U.S. five years or less are proficient. By contrast, more than half (55%) of immigrants who have lived in the U.S. for 20 years or more are proficient English speakers.

Among immigrants ages 5 and older, Spanish is the most commonly spoken language. Some 43% of immigrants in the U.S. speak Spanish at home. The top five languages spoken at home among immigrants outside of Spanish are English only (16%), followed by Chinese (6%), Hindi (5%), Filipino/Tagalog (4%) and French (3%).

How Many Immigrants Have Been Deported Recently?

Around 340,000 immigrants were deported from the U.S. in fiscal 2016, slightly up since 2015. Overall, the Obama administration deported about 3 million immigrants between 2009 and 2016, a significantly higher number than the 2 million immigrants deported by the Bush administration between 2001 and 2008.

Immigrants convicted of a crime made up the minority of deportations in 2016, the most recent year for which statistics by criminal status are available. Of the 340,000 immigrants deported in 2016, some 40% had criminal convictions and 60% were not convicted of a crime. From 2001 to 2016, a majority (60%) of immigrants deported have not been convicted of a crime.

How Many Immigrants Are Apprehended at the U.S.-Mexico Border?

The number of apprehensions at the U.S.-Mexico border has sharply decreased over the past decade or so, from more than 1 million in fiscal 2006 to 303,916 in fiscal 2017. Today, there are more apprehensions of non-Mexicans than Mexicans at the border. In fiscal 2017, apprehensions of Central Americans at the border exceeded those of Mexicans for the third time since 2014.

How Do Americans View Immigrants and Immigration?

While immigration has been at the forefront of a national political debate, the U.S. public holds a range of views about immigrants living in the country. Overall, a majority of Americans have positive views about immigrants. Six-in-ten Americans (65%) say immigrants strengthen the country "because of their hard work and talents," while just over a quarter (26%) say immigrants burden the country by taking jobs, housing and health care.

Yet these views vary starkly by political affiliation. Among Democrats and Democratic-leaning independents, 84% think immigrants strengthen the country with their hard work and talents, and just 12% say they are a burden. Among Republicans and Republican-leaning independents, roughly as many (44%) say immigrants are a burden as say immigrants strengthen the country because of their hard work and talents (42%).

Americans also hold more positive views of some immigrant groups than others, according to a 2015 Pew Research Center immigration report. More than four-in-ten Americans expressed mostly positive views of Asian (47%) and European immigrants (44%), yet only a quarter expressed such views of African and Latin American immigrants (26% each). Roughly half of the U.S. public said immigrants are making things better through food, music and the arts (49%), but almost equal shares said immigrants are making crime and the economy worse (50% each).

Americans were divided on future levels of immigration. Nearly half said immigration to the U.S. should be decreased (49%), while one-third (34%) said immigration should be kept at its present level and just 15% said immigration should be increased.

> *"First generation Mexican immigrants are 45% less likely to commit a violent offence than third generation Americans."*

In Most Cases, Immigrants Are Not to Blame for High Crime Rates

Dainis Ignatans

In the following viewpoint, Dainis Ignatans argues that despite popular belief, geographic areas with a high proportion of recent immigrants are less likely to have crime. He contends that if immigrants settle in neighborhoods of similar culture, crime will be less likely. He also notes that among refugees seeking asylum in the United Kingdom, crime is more likely. Where culture clashes exist, there will be more crime. Dainis Ignatans is an immigrant to the United Kingdom from Latvia. He is a senior lecturer in criminology at the University of Huddlesfield.

As you read, consider the following questions:

1. What is the effect of culture clash on immigrant crime rates?
2. What two reactions rise with increased immigration?
3. Which type of immigrants are overrepresented in German and Danish crime rates?

"Immigration and Crime, Is There a Link?" by Dainis Ignatans, The Conversation, 04/10/2018. https://theconversation.com/immigration-and-crime-is-there-a-link-93521.

I am an immigrant. Many people worry about those like me, and those from other countries who might follow in my footsteps.

Bold newspaper headlines either blame immigrants for a whole host of issues or portray them as saintly helpers in the struggle for economic well-being.

Political parties use immigration policies as key selling points, driving a division in public opinion—with either fear and hostility towards immigrants, or with unnecessary overwhelming praise. Both are equally undeserved.

And in this politically charged atmosphere, discussion of immigration has become the poster child of an era in which expertise is vilified and inconvenient truths become "fake news." And the fewer facts we have, the more outrage there is.

A Mixed Picture

The reality is that as researchers, we know little about the relationship, if any, between immigration and crime. This is in part because lowbrow journalistic obsession with immigration and crime has made it somewhat a taboo topic for research. As evidenced by the limited academic literature available, a consensus simply does not exist.

In the US, areas with higher concentrations of recent immigrants have been found to actually have reduced levels of homicide and robbery. Using police recorded data in Chicago, researchers also found that first generation Mexican immigrants are 45% less likely to commit a violent offence than third generation Americans.

Similarly, a large scale European study on the effects of immigration on crime concluded that while an increase in immigration generally does not affect crime levels, it does go hand-in-hand with increased public anxiety and anti-immigration stances.

It's All About Culture

Research also shows that immigrants who come from culturally similar backgrounds to their new area, are likely to commit fewer crimes than the native population. Research on Los Angeles, for example, found that a higher number of Latino immigrants who were from culturally similar regions to the current residents, reduced the rates of violence in the area.

Similarly, research in Spain showed that Spanish speaking immigrants had a much more benign impact on crime than those of other origins. Such immigrants undoubtedly have an easier time moving to a new country where the culture reflects something like their own.

And yet, people from ethnic minority groups in Western countries are disproportionately likely to be arrested and imprisoned for most crime types. And asylum seekers are over-represented in the crime figures in Germany and Denmark.

Similarly in the UK, the impact of two waves of immigration has been examined by researchers, specifically looking at the relationship between a rise in immigration and crime levels. The analysis found that when workers from Eastern European states (that joined the EU in 2004) came to the UK, the impact on crime was minimal. But the research also found that the wave of asylum seekers who came to the UK in the 1990s— mainly from war torn countries such as Iraq, Afghanistan, and Somalia—coincided with a slight increase in the total number of property crimes at the time. This was thought to be down to the fact that employment rates for this wave of immigrants was much lower than those of the average Briton.

What About Multicultural Areas?

Immigrant populations tend to be very concentrated, with people tending to reside in areas with existing communities. My recent research shows that throughout England and Wales, areas where immigrants from one single background make up a significant majority of the immigrant population, tend to be low in crime. Nearly as low in crime as the areas with small immigrant populations.

It doesn't make a difference what the background of the immigrant population is, what appears to be key is that there is a cultural similarity among the immigrant population within an area. My research also found that areas with very high numbers of immigrants that are low in crime—or below the nation's average —tend to be areas with either European or African immigrants.

But my research also showed that areas where two or more cultures (other than that of the indigenous population) are prevalent, tend to be very high in crime. This is specifically the case in areas with the highest proportions of immigrants from Asia and Europe. In these areas violent crime is 70% higher, property crime is 92% higher and vehicle crime increases by 19% compared to national average.

What to Do About It

The research I have carried out shows the need to view culture as invaluable in the examination of the impact immigration has on crime.

It must also be considered that immigrant communities are less inclined to contact police and more likely to "self police"—which inevitably can result in more crime. So, policing of immigrant communities, which are becoming increasingly more concentrated, needs to be done with cultural differences in mind.

Social housing and other affordable housing initiatives must also be thought through carefully to avoid creating cultural clashes where possible. Some recent advances such as the UK government's Integrated Communities Strategy already try to address language barriers that preclude integration. But ultimately, more calm discussion with a view towards a safer and more cohesive world would not hurt either.

> *"But the vast majority of crimes (more than 90 percent) are dealt with at the state and local level, where those kinds of data are harder to come by because those jurisdictions rarely record whether prisoners are immigrants in the country illegally."*

We Simply Are Not Sure If Immigrants Increase Crime Rates

Robert Farley

In the following viewpoint, Robert Farley argues that evidence exists on both sides of the debate whether illegal immigrants in the United States are linked to increased crime rates. Undocumented immigrants are more likely to be sentenced for federal crimes, but that may be because the Justice Department tracks it. According to a study of Texas crimes by the Cato Institute and expert interviews, Farley shows that President Trump has misused crime statistics. The Cato study indicates illegal immigrants perpetrate far fewer crimes than Americans. Yet the truth is, there is not enough good data, but plenty of contradictory information, to make a strong conclusion either way. Robert Farley is deputy managing editor at FactCheck.org.

"Is Illegal Immigration Linked to More or Less Crime?" by Robert Farley, FactCheck.org, a project of the Annenberg Public Policy Center, June 27, 2018. Reprinted by permission.

As you read, consider the following questions:

1. What percentage of crimes occur at the state and local level?
2. In Texas in 2015, how many native-born Americans were arrested? Legal immigrants? Illegal immigrants?
3. What did the Census Bureau's American Community Survey for 2016 conclude about immigrants and crime?

President Donald Trump said it's "not true" that immigrants in the U.S. illegally are "safer than the people that live in the country," providing several crime statistics he claimed represented the "toll of illegal immigration." Sen. Bernie Sanders made the opposite claim, saying: "I understand that the crime rate among undocumented people is actually lower than the general population."

Who is right?

There are not readily available nationwide statistics on all crimes committed by immigrants in the country illegally. Researchers have provided estimates through statistical modeling or by extrapolating from smaller samples. One such study backs the president's claim, but several others support Sanders' statement.

Trump made his claim during a press conference on June 22 with "angel families" whose loved ones were killed by immigrants without legal status. Trump sought to debunk the idea that immigrants who come to the country illegally have lower rates of violent crime than native-born Americans. But he rattled off government statistics on various crimes committed by all immigrants in an attempt to make his point.

> Trump, June 22: So here are just a few statistics on the human toll of illegal immigration. According to a 2011 government report, the arrests attached to the criminal alien population included an estimated 25,000 people for homicide, 42,000 for robbery, nearly 70,000 for sex offenses, and nearly 15,000 for kidnapping. In Texas alone, within the last seven years, more

than a quarter million criminal aliens have been arrested and charged with over 600,000 criminal offenses. You don't hear that.

I always hear that, "Oh, no, the population's safer than the people that live in the country." You've heard that, fellas, right? You've heard that. I hear it so much, and I say, "Is that possible?" The answer is it's not true. You hear it's like they're better people than what we have, than our citizens. It's not true.

Two days after Trump made his remarks, Sanders responded on CNN's "State of the Union," saying that the crime rate for those in the country illegally "is actually lower than the general population."

The issue is ripe for dispute because, as we said, there are not readily available statistics on this issue. The Justice Department keeps data on federal crimes committed by immigrants in the country illegally—and an analysis from the U.S. Sentencing Commission found that undocumented immigrants made up a disproportionate share of federal inmates sentenced for nonimmigration crimes in 2016. But the vast majority of crimes (more than 90 percent) are dealt with at the state and local level, where those kinds of data are harder to come by because those jurisdictions rarely record whether prisoners are immigrants in the country illegally.

Trump's Case

In making his case, Trump did not cite any kind of study that attempts to show whether illegal immigration is associated with more crime. Rather, he provided statistics on the number of crimes committed by all noncitizens, whether they are in the country illegally or legally.

The first set of numbers on homicides, robberies, sex offenses and kidnappings nationwide come from a Government Accountability Office report in 2011 (https://www.gao.gov/new. items/d11187.pdf; see Table 2 on page 21) based on FBI arrest histories of all immigrants incarcerated in local jails and state and federal prisons. The figures include arrests of "criminal aliens," which are all noncitizens, between August 1955 and April 2010, though about 90 percent of the arrests were after 1990. The report does not compare the crime rates of immigrants in the country illegally with those for native-born residents.

The Texas numbers cited by Trump come from the state Department of Public Safety, and Trump has inaccurately cited the state's figures before. They, too, are for arrests for all noncitizens, even though the state does give some figures for arrests of those identified as being in the country illegally. Still, the state agency acknowledges that its figures "do not attempt to allege that foreign nationals in the country illegally commit more crimes than other groups."

Research Showing Lower Crime Rates

Alex Nowrasteh, with the libertarian Cato Institute, analyzed the Texas data to make a comparison of immigrants in the country illegally and native-born residents. In a recent post he noted that in 2015 Texas police made 815,689 arrests of native-born Americans, 37,776 arrests of immigrants in the country illegally and 20,323 arrests of legal immigrants. Given the relative populations for each group, he wrote, "The arrest rate for illegal immigrants was 40 percent below that of native-born Americans."

In addition, he wrote, the homicide arrest rate for native-born Americans was "about 46 percent higher than the illegal immigrant homicide arrest rate."

Other research from the Cato Institute attempted to provide national estimates. A study published on June 4 used data from the Census Bureau's American Community Survey for 2016 and applied statistical modeling to estimate the number of incarcerated immigrants in the country illegally. It filtered the data using characteristics correlated with being an immigrant in the country illegally, such as whether someone is a noncitizen but has not served in the military or received Social Security income. The research concluded: "Illegal immigrants are 47 percent less likely to be incarcerated than natives." (And legal immigrants are even less likely to be in jail or prison.)

Cato, June 4: If native-born Americans were incarcerated at the same rate as illegal immigrants, about 930,000 fewer natives would be incarcerated. Conversely, if natives were incarcerated at the same rate as legal immigrants, about 1.5 million fewer natives would be in adult correctional facilities.

Another study, "Does Undocumented Immigration Increase Violent Crime?," which was published in the journal Criminology in March, looked at the influx of undocumented immigrants into communities in recent decades and concluded, "Increased concentrations of undocumented immigrants are associated with statistically significant decreases in violent crime."

One of the study's authors, Michael Light, a professor of sociology and Chicano/Latino studies at the University of Wisconsin, told us via email that the president is conflating two different issues and misusing statistics.

"The claim that immigrants are less crime prone refers exactly to the type of findings [from his study and the one from Cato]: that the rate of crime within the immigrant community is lower than the rate of crime among U.S. citizens. OR, that communities with high levels of immigrants tend to have lower crime rates than communities with fewer immigrants," Light said. "And those statements are not contradicted by stating the number of offenses committed by immigrants (as the President did)."

"Imagine I were to claim that women are less violent than men, which is as close to a social fact that we have in criminology," Light said. "And one were to reply saying that this isn't true because in 2015 over 78,000 women were arrested for violent crimes, and nearly 1,000 were arrested for homicide. Those statistics in no way contradict the original statement that men tend to be more violent."

Research published in Social Science Quarterly in 2016 looked at rates of violent crime and drug arrests by state for 2012 to 2014 and compared them with statistics on the foreign-born and Mexican nationals living in the United States, as well as estimates of the undocumented foreign and undocumented Mexican population by state. The study found no association between immigrant population size and increased violent crime, though it found a "small but significant association between undocumented immigrant populations and drug-related arrests."

Interestingly, a Pew Research Center report in 2013 found that crime rates rise among second-generation immigrants, more closely mirroring the rates of other native-born residents. Some researchers say this is a result of assimilation and simply "catching-up" to their peers.

Numerous other studies have found that immigrants overall— including those with legal status—do not commit crimes at a higher rate than non-immigrants, and that higher concentrations of immigrants do not lead to higher rates of violent crime. A recap of the literature on this topic can be found here. But those studies don't look specifically at illegal immigration.

Conflicting Research

There is, however, one study that backs the president's claim. John Lott, president of the Crime Prevention Research Center, looked at data on prisoners in Arizona state prison between the beginning of 1985 and June 2017 and concluded that "undocumented immigrants are at least 146% more likely to be convicted of crime than other Arizonans." They also tend to commit more serious crimes, and have significantly higher rates for such crimes as murder, manslaughter, sexual assault and armed robbery, Lott concluded, and are more likely to be gang members. Conversely, Lott found that legal immigrants "were extremely law-abiding," committing crimes at a lower rate than native-born residents.

Although Lott says his study is unique because "for the first time" he was able to differentiate between immigrants in the country legally and illegally, that claim was contested by Nowrasteh of the Cato Institute. Nowrasteh argues Lott's study contains a "fatal flaw" in its assumption that it was able to "identify illegal immigrants" from the data. The *Washington Post* Fact Checker did a deep dive on the arguments and counterarguments about the validity of the study.

"The overall picture of immigrants and crime remains confused due to a lack of good data and contrary information," Steven Camarota and Jessica Vaughan of the Center for Immigration Studies, a group that advocates low immigration, wrote in 2009.

Camarota told us it is somewhat irrelevant whether immigrants in the country illegally commit crimes at a slightly higher or lower rate than native-born Americans.

"Does releasing illegal immigrants allow them to commit crimes they otherwise would not have committed, yes it does," Camarota told us in an email. "Do the crimes committed by released illegal immigrants number in the thousands, yes they do."

But we are looking at a claim from Trump about the comparison of crime rates of immigrants in the country illegally and native-born residents.

"If you are asking if illegals commit crimes out of their proportion of the population as I said maybe, maybe not," Camarota said. "Data is limited and it depends on who you compare them to."

As we said, there aren't readily available nationwide crime statistics broken down by immigration status. But the available research that estimates the relationship between illegal immigration and crime generally shows an association with lower crime rates. The impetus is on the president to provide evidence of his claim, and Trump instead simply cited statistics on violent crime committed by all noncitizens without attempting to compare those figures to crimes committed by native-born residents.

> "[The bill] declares English as the
> official language of the United States
> and will help set legal immigrants
> on a path to success as they integrate
> and work towards becoming citizens.
> As a nation built by immigrants, this
> legislation will strengthen the cords
> of unity that comes from sharing one
> vision and one official language."

The English Language Unity Act Would Make English the Official US Language

GovTrack Insider

In the following viewpoint, GovTrack Insider explains H.R. 997 and S. 678, also known as the English Language Unity Act. This legislation would make English the official language of the United States. As explained by the cosponsors, if immigrants were required to become proficient in the national language, they would better understand their rights, would be more likely to become engaged members of society, and would generally be in a better position to achieve success in their adopted country. However, opponents believe legislation is unnecessary. At the time of this writing, the English Language Unity Act has been referred by the Senate to the Committee on Homeland Security and Government Affairs. GovTrack Insider is a website that tracks bills and members of US Congress.

As you read, consider the following questions:

1. How many people in the United States speak a language other than English in their homes?
2. Who are the cosponsors of the English Language Unity Act?
3. What did President Obama say was equally important as immigrants learning English?

An estimated 21.1 percent of U.S. residents now speak a language other than English at home, according to the U.S. Census Bureau. That's 63.2 million residents, approximately doubled since 1990 and tripled since 1980. Some members of Congress see this as a worrying sign or even a threat.

Rep. Steve King (R-IA4) and Sen. Jim Inhofe (R-OK) are two such members. Together they've introduced H.R. 997 and S. 678, the English Language Unity Act, in the House and Senate. The legislation would declare English the official language of the United States and require that all people attempting to become citizens show English language proficiency.

What Supporters Say

Supporters say the legislation would create a common bond and prevent miscommunication. They also note that 31 states have adopted English as the official language, including many Democrat-leaning states.

"There is no more unifying force in the world than a common form of communications currency," King said in a press release announcing the bill. "Every sovereign nation state, including the Vatican, has at a minimum, an official language. It is essential that we make assimilation of our legal immigrants a top priority and learning English is an important first step in that process.

"The United States' culturally diverse population is what makes our nation great, and what helps us move forward together as a society is the ability to communicate to one another," said Inhofe

THREE REASONS WHY IMMIGRANTS SHOULD LEARN ENGLISH

Understanding English in a predominantly English-speaking country allows immigrants to get better-paying jobs. According to the Census Bureau, about 5 million native-born Americans have limited English skills. An additional 20 million foreign-born US residents can't speak English "very well." This lack of facility with English is one of the major reasons many immigrants turn to jobs that don't require extensive language skills—migrant work, for instance—and that means far lower pay than they need to take care of themselves and their families.

Not learning English can lead to social isolation. Immigrants often form separate communities more easily navigated by their native languages even after they've moved to an English-speaking country. While maintaining one's culture of origin is important, doing it to the exclusion of all else can create tension and limited opportunities to fully benefit from a new country and all it has to offer.

Lack of engagement with an adopted culture can lead to violence and extremism.

UK Labor MP Chuka Umunna noted that "the Government has a duty to address the lack of integration of immigrants....Failing to do so has left a vacuum for extremists and peddlers of hate to exploit." If an immigrant doesn't feel like a fully integrated member of their new society, it's easier for them to be swayed by those promoting terrorism and other violent behavior. Learning the predominantly spoken language is one way to create a sense of connection and ownership when it comes to community.

"Why Immigrants Should Learn English," by Martin Ackerman, Industry Buzz, April 13, 2017.

in his own press release. "[The bill] declares English as the official language of the United States and will help set legal immigrants on a path to success as they integrate and work towards becoming citizens. As a nation built by immigrants, this legislation will strengthen the cords of unity that comes from sharing one vision and one official language."

What Opponents Say

Opponents argue that the legislation is an attack on the melting pot diversity of both the languages and nationalities that make our country great, and that in practice English will always be far and away the predominant language in America whether or not it's official.

President Obama, who has said when asked about the question that "I agree that immigrants should learn English," said that a law was unnecessary and could even be hypocritical. Many Americans "go over to Europe, and all we can say is 'merci beaucoup,'" Obama said. "Instead of worrying about whether immigrants can learn English—they'll learn English—you need to make sure your child can speak Spanish. You should be thinking about how can your child become bilingual. We should have every child speaking more than one language."

The bill makes exceptions to permit federal government use of other languages in cases including national security, international relations, tourism, public safety and health, and "protecting the rights of victims."

Odds of Passage

The long-standing anti-immigration positions of the Republican party might create the impression that there is a groundswell of support for this type of legislation, but while the Senate bill has been gaining more cosponsors over the years, the House bill has actually consistently declined in recent years, as measured by cosponsors and bipartisanship. The current House bill has 90 cosponsors and no Democrats, representing a decrease and less bipartisanship than the version introduced in the previous Congress: 94 cosponsors, including two Democrats.

Going back further, the prior versions in Congress had even more cosponsors and were more bipartisan: 112 cosponsors, including four Democrats; before that 138 cosponsors, including seven Democrats; before that 153 cosponsors, including seven

Democrats; before that 164 cosponsors, including six Democrats. None of the bills ever received a vote.

In the Senate, he seven cosponsors is more than the six cosponsors for the previous version, three cosponsors for the version before that, and again three cosponsors for the version before that. (All were Republican every year.) Those bills never received votes either.

The current legislation is pending before the House Education and the Workforce or House Judiciary Committees and the Senate Homeland Security and Governmental Affairs Committee.

> "*One reason the lawyers are worried is that they've seen a barrage of scrutiny directed at once-standard immigration applications since Trump took office.*"

Strict Immigration Policies Hurt US Employers

Kavitha Surana

In the following viewpoint, Kavitha Surana argues that President Trump's attempts to cut down on immigration, includes both legal and illegal immigrants. USCIS officers now can deny visa or green card applications for a minor error. This will hurt immigrants coming to the United States with H-1B work visas and will affect their employers, too. Before the president took office USCIS officers allowed immigrants to correct these areas. Kavitha Surana is a senior reporting fellow at ProPublica, where she writes about immigration. She previously wrote for Foreign Policy *magazine, covering immigration, border security policy, and counterterrorism.*

As you read, consider the following questions:

1. What is the H-1B visa category?
2. According to this viewpoint, what is the "invisible wall?"
3. What action did a group of corporate chief executive officers (CEOs) take?

As President Donald Trump wages a vocal battle against illegal immigration, his administration has been working more quietly to cut down on legal pathways to immigrate to the U.S.

On Tuesday, a new policy kicks in, allowing officers with the U.S. Citizenship and Immigration Services to outright deny any visa or green card application that is missing evidence or contains an error. Around 7 million people apply every year.

Previously, officers were required by an Obama-era policy to send notices, giving applicants a chance to correct such problems instead of closing the process. Officers can still choose to do so, but they can also opt to skip that step if the application is deemed frivolous.

Without the notices, applicants won't have the opportunity to intervene before a decision is made, potentially adding months or years of extra paperwork and thousands of dollars in fees to the already lengthy process. In the case of those trying to renew their visas while they're still in the U.S., they could be placed in deportation proceedings the moment their visas expire.

USCIS spokesman Michael Bars said the policy was changed to cut down on frivolous applications. The agency has said applicants sometimes file substantially incomplete placeholder applications, knowing the back-and-forth with the USCIS will buy them time. "Under the law, the burden of proof is on the applicant," Bars said, "not the other way around."

But immigration lawyers worry that there is not enough oversight or clear standards to ensure fair handling. USCIS officers will now have near-complete discretion to make complex judgments behind closed doors.

"They can deny you on the fact that, subjectively, they feel in their mind [the application] is not approvable," Pierre Bonnefil, an immigration attorney in New York, said.

One reason the lawyers are worried is that they've seen a barrage of scrutiny directed at once-standard immigration applications since Trump took office. ProPublica spoke with a dozen lawyers and reviewed documentation for several of these cases.

Many responses cited technicalities: One application was not accepted because the seventh page, usually left blank, was not attached. Another was rejected because it did not have a table of contents and exhibit numbers, even though it had other forms of organization.

"It seems like they are just making every single submission difficult," Bonnefil said. "Even the most standard, run-of-the-mill" application."

The lawyers call this minefield of onerous paperwork an "invisible wall," designed to make legal immigration as difficult as possible.

"People who are here legally, doing everything through proper channels, now feel as unsettled and unwelcome and uncertain about the future as people who don't have documents," Sandra Feist, an immigration attorney in Minnesota, said.

Under Trump, this has meant that cases drag on for weeks or months as lawyers scramble to address notices. Some lawyers have noticed an uptick in denials recently, but most say that strong cases still eventually make it through.

It remains to be seen how broadly the new policy will be used to outright deny even strong applications. The memo said the new policy is "not intended to penalize filers for innocent mistakes or misunderstandings of evidentiary requirements."

Apart from technicalities, lawyers have noted an increase in detailed requests for evidence. Some of the new questions fit with Trump's 2017 Executive Order called "Buy American and Hire American," which directed the Department of Homeland Security to find ways to make sure specialty work visas are awarded only to the most highly skilled and highest-paid foreign workers, to fill jobs that couldn't be filled by an American.

To some, the increased scrutiny of work visas is welcome.

In particular, the H-1B visa category has often been the subject of controversy. Intended for high-level workers with specialized skills, it has been used to outsource ordinary jobs. In 2014, for example, Disney laid off about 250 long-time workers in computer jobs so that they could replace them with workers flown in from India. The Americans were required to train their replacements before they left. A federal court found that Disney did not violate any laws and the case was eventually dropped, but Republicans have often pointed to similar cases to call for tougher oversight of foreign worker programs.

"It's almost like it's a subclass of employee that they can take advantage of and can work them extra hard for smaller pay," said Rennie Sawade, the communications chair of the Washington Alliance of Technology Workers. He has experienced increased competition in his own search for jobs in the tech industry and in that of his son, who is 24 and has an associate degree in robotics and computer networking but is still struggling to find work. "These visas should be used for what they are intended for, so you definitely need more scrutiny in how they are being used."

But lawyers argue the stepped-up examinations go beyond what's required to assess an immigrant's eligibility and seem intended to simply make the process more burdensome for all immigrants. Under Trump, the extra layer of questions has not been limited to H-1B cases, but applied to all types of work visas, family-based green cards and humanitarian cases. The extra questions are also directed toward people who have lived and worked in the U.S. for more than a decade and are applying to extend their visas.

Foreign workers once considered to have slam-dunk immigration cases—an internationally recognized physicist, an Alzheimer's disease researcher, a biologist doing "cutting edge" work on vaccine development—are now finding themselves tied up in extra requests for evidence to prove their skills are truly specialized.

One Iranian professor, in the process of launching a graduate degree program at an American university, included 10 letters of recommendation from experts in his field and evidence of his awards and publications. Feist, his lawyer, said she felt certain his petition for a green card under the "outstanding professor" category would sail through.

Instead, she received a notice of intent to deny, reviewed by ProPublica, pointing out a slew of quibbles: The professor had published frequently in his field, but was he cited often enough? He had won awards, but the reviewing officer didn't think they were truly prestigious. The professor had served on panels and presented at conferences, but those were not really sufficient to prove influence, the officer wrote.

"This is just one example of pretty typical aggressive requests for additional evidence that I'm seeing that are far outside of the norm that I've seen in the past 17 years," Feist said.

Michael Cataliotti, an immigration lawyer in New York, recalled a case in which he printed and attached emails between a physicist and the editors of peer-reviewed journals, to demonstrate the physicist had served as a reviewer for each of them. Because the email was printed from his work computer, Cataliotti's name appeared at the top of the paper.

This seemed to confuse the USCIS official handling the case. "The document has been altered, and as such, is inadmissible," the official wrote.

Other examples show an overly strict reading of the rules, sometimes applied incorrectly. Courtney Morgan-Greene, an immigration attorney in California, said the USCIS tried to deny a religious worker's request for a visa extension because she had taken some time off from her job—in order to give birth, and then to mourn the death of her child after 11 months.

The response from the agency began, "While USCIS sympathizes with the death of the beneficiary's baby," and went on to deny the case based on the time she took off. Morgan-Greene emailed the quote to ProPublica.

USCIS policy allows breaks in employment "such as sick leave, pregnancy leave, spousal care and vacation as long as they do not exceed two years." Morgan-Greene said her client's two periods of leave combined did not add up to two years. "Not only is the decision incorrect as a matter of law, it shocks the conscience," she said.

Employers are just as frustrated as immigrants trying to obtain green cards and visas. On Aug. 22, a group of CEOs representing major U.S. companies, including JPMorgan Chase, Cisco Systems, American Airlines, Apple, Coca-Cola and Texas Instruments, sent a letter to DHS Secretary Kirstjen Nielsen with their concerns with recent USCIS policy changes.

"Inconsistent government action and uncertainty undermines economic growth and American competitiveness and creates anxiety for employees who follow the law," they wrote.

They added: "USCIS actions significantly increase the likelihood that a long-term employee—who has followed the rules and who has been authorized by the U.S. government multiple times to work in the United States—will lose his or her status. All of this despite the Department of Labor having, in many cases, certified that no qualified U.S. workers are available to do that person's job."

Sarah Pierce, a policy analyst at the Migration Policy Institute, said examples of H-1B misuse are "highly concerning," but she said that there's no clear data to prove how widespread it is. "We know there are a lot of legitimate employers that use this program as well," she said.

Pierce said targeted approaches—such as limiting contractors from hiring H-1B workers or going after companies that mainly depend on H-1B workers—would be better solutions than a blanket approach making it difficult for all companies to hire foreign workers.

But Trump has made it clear that he would like to see a reduction in all immigration. "One thing really unique about

President Trump is he views not just illegal immigration, but legal immigration through the context of it being a security threat and an economic threat to the United States," Pierce said.

Even when cases are ultimately approved, Feist says employers have told her they will reconsider going through the process again. Workers stuck in limbo have told her they're considering other options, too.

Cataliotti agreed the strategy seems designed to frustrate, "so either one or both parties says: Forget it, I can't do this anymore, the position is gone, or I might as well go to Canada."

> *"We are a nation that welcomes the tired, the poor, and the huddled weary who yearn to breathe free and build a better life for their children."*

We Are a Nation of Immigrants Who Were All Strangers Once

Tanya Somanader

In the following viewpoint, Tanya Somanader argues that during the Obama administration, the president recognized that the immigration system was broken. Addressing the nation on November 20, 2014, Obama outlined a number of executive actions he would take to repair that system. These actions included more law enforcement staff at the border, easing the process for high-skilled immigrants and graduate students to immigrate, and to deal responsibly with illegal immigrants. Tanya Somanader is former Director of Rapid Response for the Office of Digital Strategy for the White House. She is now chief content officer for Crooked Media in Los Angeles.

As you read, consider the following questions:

1. Prior to this speech, what reduction in illegal border crossings occurred?
2. How does Obama define amnesty?
3. What is the American shared commitment to an ideal?

"'We Were Strangers Once, Too': The President Announces New Steps on Immigration," by Tanya Somanader, The White House, November 20, 2014.

S ince the founding of our nation, we've weaved a tradition of welcoming immigrants into the very fabric of who we are. It's what keeps us dynamic, entrepreneurial, and uniquely American.

But, as we know all too well, America's immigration system is broken. So tonight, President Obama addressed the nation on the executive actions he is taking to help fix what he can:

1. We will build on our progress at the border with additional resources for our law enforcement personnel.

Today, we have more agents and technology deployed to secure our southern border than at any time in our history. And over the past six years, illegal border crossings have been cut by more than half. Although this summer, there was a brief spike in unaccompanied children being apprehended at our border, the number of such children is now actually lower than it's been in nearly two years. Overall, the number of people trying to cross our border illegally is at its lowest level since the 1970s. Those are the facts.

2. We will make it easier and faster for high-skilled immigrants, graduates, and entrepreneurs to stay and contribute to our economy, as so many business leaders have proposed.

3. We will take steps to deal responsibly with the millions of undocumented immigrants who already live in our country.

Families who enter our country the right way and play by the rules watch others flout the rules. Business owners who offer their workers good wages and benefits see the competition exploit undocumented immigrants by paying them far less. All of us take offense to anyone who reaps the rewards of living in America without taking on the responsibilities of living in America. And undocumented immigrants who desperately want to embrace those responsibilities see little option but to remain in the shadows, or risk their families being torn apart.

We are a nation of immigrants, and we are a nation of laws. We must hold accountable those who broke the law, while understanding that the mass deportation of millions of Americans is neither possible nor in keeping with who we are as Americans. That is why the President is focusing enforcement resources on actual threats to our security: "Felons, not families. Criminals, not children. Gang members, not a mom who's working hard to provide for her kids."

So here is the deal the President put forward tonight:

> If you've been in America for more than five years; if you have children who are American citizens or legal residents; if you register, pass a criminal background check, and you're willing to pay your fair share of taxes—you'll be able to apply to stay in this country temporarily, without fear of deportation. You can come out of the shadows and get right with the law.

Here is what this deal is not: Amnesty. Amnesty is the immigration system we have now, in which millions of people live here without paying their taxes or playing by the rules, and politicians use this issue to scare and divide Americans.

> That's the real amnesty—leaving this broken system the way it is. Mass amnesty would be unfair. Mass deportation would be both impossible and contrary to our character. What I'm describing is accountability—a common-sense, middle ground approach: If you meet the criteria, you can come out of the shadows and get right with the law. If you're a criminal, you'll be deported. If you plan to enter the U.S. illegally, your chances of getting caught and sent back just went up.

The best and most definitive way to fix the system is to pass comprehensive and common-sense immigration reform in Congress. Last year, 68 Democrats, Republicans, and independents in the Senate came together to do just that. That bipartisan bill would have doubled the number of Border Patrol agents; given undocumented immigrants a pathway to citizenship if they pay a fine, start paying taxes, and go to the back of the line; and boosted our economy while shrinking the deficit.

But more than 500 days later, Republicans in the House continue to block the bipartisan bill from a vote. "Had the House of Representatives allowed that kind of a bill a simple yes-or-no vote, it would have passed with support from both parties, and today it would be the law," the President noted.

So the President had to act, just as every president since President Eisenhower has over this last half century.

> To those Members of Congress who question my authority to make our immigration system work better, or question the wisdom of me acting where Congress has failed, I have one answer: Pass a bill.

At the heart of the President's actions is a commitment to who we are as a nation. We are a nation that values families and works together to keep them together. We are a nation that educates the world's best and brightest, and encourages them to stay and create jobs here.

We are a nation that welcomes the tired, the poor, and the huddled weary who yearn to breathe free and build a better life for their children.

As the President said:

> Scripture tells us that we shall not oppress a stranger, for we know the heart of a stranger—we were strangers once, too.
>
> My fellow Americans, we are and always will be a nation of immigrants. We were strangers once, too. And whether our forebears were strangers who crossed the Atlantic, or the Pacific, or the Rio Grande, we are here only because this country welcomed them in, and taught them that to be an American is about something more than what we look like, or what our last names are, or how we worship. What makes us Americans is our shared commitment to an ideal—that all of us are created equal, and all of us have the chance to make of our lives what we will.

Periodical and Internet Sources Bibliography

The following articles have been selected to supplement the diverse views presented in this chapter.

Nigel Barber, "Immigrants Are the Lifeblood of Economies," *Psychology Today*, July 10, 2018. www.psychologytoday.com/us/blog/the-human-beast/201807/immigrants-are-the-lifeblood-economies.

George J. Borjas. "Yes, Immigration Hurts American Workers," Politico, September/October 2016. www.politico.com/magazine/story/2016/09/trump-clinton-immigration-economy-unemployment-jobs-214216.

Anna Flagg, "The Myth of the Criminal Immigrant." *New York Times,* March 30, 2018. www.nytimes.com/interactive/2018/03/30/upshot/crime-immigration-myth.html.

Gretchen Frazee, "4 Myths about How Immigrants Affect the U.S. Economy," PBS, November 2, 2018. www.pbs.org/newshour/economy/making-sense/4-myths-about-how-immigrants-affect-the-u-s-economy.

Ali Imran, "Immigrant Entrepreneurs Founded 43% of 2017 Fortune 500 Companies," Views & News, December 18, 2017. www.viewsnews.net/2017/12/18/immigrant-entrepreneurs-founded-43-2017-fortune-500-companies/.

Priya Konings, "Protecting Immigrant Children's Right to Education," American Bar Association, March 1, 2017. www.americanbar.org/groups/child_law/resources/child_law_practiceonline/child_law_practice/vol-36/mar-apr-2017/protecting-immigrant-childrens-right-to-education-/.

Dan Kosten, "Immigrants as Economic Contributors: Immigrant Entrepreneurs," National Immigration Forum. July 11, 2018. immigrationforum.org/article/immigrants-as-economic-contributors-immigrant-entrepreneurs/.

Noah Smith, "Immigrants Are Making the U.S. Economy Stronger," Bloomberg Opinion, March 24, 2017. https://www.bloomberg.com/opinion/articles/2017-03-24/immigrants-are-making-the-u-s-economy-stronger.

OPPOSING VIEWPOINTS® SERIES

CHAPTER 4

Should DACA and Dreamers Be Allowed to Continue?

Chapter Preface

Since 2001, the Development, Relief, and Education for Alien Minors (DREAM) Act has stirred the American government and people. The act called for the protection of illegal immigrants who were brought into the country as children from deportation. The bill did not pass. However, in 2012, President Obama issued an executive order to enact the Deferred Action for Children Act (DACA). Some political leaders claim President Obama did not have the authority to do that. By the same reasoning, others claim President Trump also did not have the authority to end DACA through executive order.

Those who support the continuation of DACA argue that President Trump has been using DACA as a bargaining chip to get Mexico to pay for the border wall. One federal court judge ruled against ending the act and gave Trump and the Department of Homeland Security ninety days to explain the rationale. Those who oppose the continuation believe that stopping DACA will also end human trafficking and illegal drugs brought into the country. Further, there is evidence that less than half of DACA beneficiaries go beyond high school and less than half achieve more than a basic level of English competency.

State leaders have considered and brought into the courts the idea of allowing illegal immigrants in-state tuition rates. However, this puts native-born students at a disadvantage and some have filed a lawsuit to protect their own interests. Some maintain that illegal immigrants, especially the children, are entitled to certain rights, for instance, public schooling. Deportation to a country they have never really known is morally irresponsible, scholars argue.

The following chapter provides multiple perspectives concerning the legality of DACA and its effect on DACA beneficiaries. These viewpoints represent opposing political parties, federal courts, state actions, student actions, and the checks and balances of the federal government.

"The ruling could end up reanimating DACA in full, against the administration's wishes. Or it could give the administration a lifeline that will help it persuade appeals courts to overturn the defeats it's already suffered. It all depends on what happens in the next 90 days."

The President Is Determined to End DACA, but It's Not Proving Easy

Dara Lind

In the following viewpoint Dara Lind argues that DACA is getting caught up in legal red tape. The author reports on a federal judge's ruling to continue DACA, despite President Trump's efforts to eliminate the program. The decision did not fully shut down Trump's ending of DACA, but rather gave his administration 90 days to come up with a better argument on which to base its reasoning for ending the program. Since then, the fate of DACA holders is unclear. The administration rejected all legislative efforts but continued to try to overturn court orders. The Supreme Court did not take on the case for its Spring 2019 season, which meant that the two lower court rulings allowing DACA holders to renew their status are maintained. It remains to be seen whether the Supreme Court will accept the DACA case for a future season. Dara Lind is senior correspondent for Vox. She has covered immigration issues for a decade.

"A judge just opened the door to restarting DACA. Here's what his ruling means," by Dara Lind, Vox Media, April 25, 2018. Reprinted by permission.

As you read, consider the following questions:

1. According to the viewpoint, what was it about the Trump administration's argument against DACA that set off red flags for Judge Bates?
2. How many days was Trump's administration given to change their argument?
3. Who does the decision rest with for revising the argument, according to the viewpoint?

A federal judge in Washington, DC, has just reopened the door a crack to young unauthorized immigrants who qualified for relief from deportation and work permits under the Deferred Action for Childhood Arrivals (DACA) program, which the Trump administration wound down in September.

But the administration has 90 days to shut that door again.

In a ruling released Tuesday night in the case *NAACP v. Trump* (combined with the case *Trustees of Princeton University v. Trump*), DC District Judge John Bates continued a streak of legal defeats the Trump administration has suffered in their attempts to end the DACA program.

Two federal judges had already issued preliminary injunctions against the administration, forcing the government to allow immigrants who already have work permits under DACA to apply for two-year renewals.

Judge Bates went further. His ruling would force the Trump administration to allow immigrants who qualify for DACA—by being between the ages of 15 and 31, having arrived in the US before 2007, being enrolled in school or having a degree, and not having a significant criminal record—to apply for work permits even if they never applied before September 2017.

Crucially, though, Bates's ruling doesn't go into effect for 90 days. In the meantime, the judge is giving the Trump administration a chance to redeem itself. If Trump's Department of Homeland Security issues a new memo in the next 90 days that offers a stronger legal argument for ending DACA than the one it's provided so far, it can avoid having to grant new DACA permits.

The ruling could end up reanimating DACA in full, against the administration's wishes. Or it could give the administration a lifeline that will help it persuade appeals courts to overturn the defeats it's already suffered. It all depends on what happens in the next 90 days.

This Ruling Changes Nothing Immediately. But It's Potentially Good News for People Who Qualify for DACA.

Immigrants who currently have a valid work permit under DACA—or who had one as of September 5, 2016, which has since expired—are currently allowed to apply for a two-year renewal of their work permit and protection from deportation. That's the result of a January court ruling from a federal judge in California, in another lawsuit against the administration. (A judge in New York, in yet another lawsuit, has subsequently ruled the same way, meaning that the Trump administration will have to overturn both rulings to stop processing renewals again.)

If Judge Bates's new ruling goes into effect in late July, though, it would go further than that. It would allow people who qualified for DACA but didn't apply for it the opportunity to apply for a two-year work permit for the first time.

And it would allow DACA recipients to apply for permission to leave the country and be allowed in when they return—allowing some DACA recipients to clear a hurdle blocking their path to full legal status they'd otherwise qualify for.

Potentially, this could affect hundreds of thousands of people—estimates indicate that as many as 1 million people qualified for DACA while it was in place but never applied for it. White House Chief of Staff John Kelly characterized them as "too lazy to get off their asses"; more likely, they couldn't afford the $495 application fee or were afraid to give the government their information. Even if the door were opened for them to apply now, those things might still be true, so it's not clear how many of the people who didn't apply before would apply now.

It might be more meaningful for the thousands of immigrants who have turned 15 since September 5—they were too young to apply for DACA while it was in place, and because the Trump administration stopped accepting new applications immediately in September, they weren't allowed to apply once they qualified. The Center for American Progress estimated that as of March 5, 23,000 immigrants had become DACA-eligible after the administration shut the door on them.

But DACA hasn't reopened yet. Bates delayed his ruling for 90 days to give the Trump administration a second chance. If the administration takes it, the ruling might never go into effect.

The Trump Administration Has 90 Days to Come Up with a Better Reason DACA Should End

The heart of Bates's legal argument is that the Trump administration claimed it had to end DACA because it was unconstitutional—but "that legal judgment was virtually unexplained," the judge wrote, "and so it cannot support the agency's decision."

For one thing, the Trump administration passed judgment on DACA's unconstitutionality before any federal judge had actually said so themselves. Federal courts put a later and broader deferred action program, one for parents of US citizens and green card holders, on ice in 2015—but DACA was explicitly not included in that ruling. And the only legal challenge against DACA itself, back in 2012 when the program was first started, was thrown out of court.

Additionally, in the lawsuits against the end of DACA, the administration is now claiming that the courts don't even have the authority to rule over its decision to rescind the program. For Bates, the fact that the administration ended DACA because it was unconstitutional but is now telling the courts that ending DACA is outside the scope of constitutional review set off red flags.

This is important because Bates isn't just rejecting the reason the Trump administration gave him. He's giving the Trump administration 90 days to come up with a better one: "The Court will stay its order of vacatur for 90 days, however, to afford DHS an opportunity to better explain its view that DACA is unlawful."

Whether the court would accept that alternate rationale is an open question—the ruling doesn't exactly set out a checklist for what an acceptable DACA rescission would look like. (This bears a resemblance to the Supreme Court case over the travel ban, which also raises questions about when, and how closely, the federal courts can scrutinize executive branch policy.)

Even if Bates did rule that the Trump administration's new argument was strong enough to let the end of DACA go forward, it wouldn't overrule the federal judges in New York and California who have forced the administration to start accepting renewals again. But it might strengthen the administration's hand as it appeals those rulings. Neither of the previous opinions relied on the argument that you can't presume something is unconstitutional, like Bates just did, but they both noted it, and it appears to have factored into their general judgments that the administration ended DACA in a rash and capricious way.

Armed with a stronger legal grounding for killing DACA due to the DC ruling, the Trump administration might force appeals courts on the coasts to take a second look at the case for ending DACA, and to consider whether the person acting rashly was not the administration but the judges who ordered renewals to start up again.

The Trump Administration Has Another Chance to Try to Kill DACA, and It Will Almost Certainly Take It

If the Trump administration finds a new reason that DACA shouldn't go back into effect, it will be incontrovertibly clear that the administration is responsible for killing the program.

In September, Trump was able to muddy the waters of political blame: While Attorney General Jeff Sessions took the "bad cop" role of formally announcing DACA's sunset, Trump tweeted false reassurances to immigrants. The president was willing to pull the trigger on ending DACA when it looked like Congress would either step in to fix it or take the blame by failing to do so.

If it were up to Trump now, maybe the Department of Homeland Security wouldn't bother to argue that DACA should be put on hold.

But it's probably not up to Trump.

Technically, the decision rests with Kirstjen Nielsen, Trump's homeland security secretary and a protégé of predecessor John Kelly (now Trump's chief of staff); like Kelly, Nielsen has gotten more comfortable in the role of immigration enforcer as she's been in the job.

Because the judge is asking specifically for a legal argument, though, the role of killing DACA again might fall to the same person who announced its death the first time: Sessions. Nielsen may not have a strong preexisting opinion that DACA needed to die. Sessions absolutely does.

Judge Bates just gave them another 90 days to make their best case, and they are all but guaranteed to take it. The question is what comes next.

> *"By promoting human trafficking, the Obama administration helped 'fund the illegal drug cartels which are a very real danger for both citizens of this country and Mexico."*

Stopping DACA Brings an End to Human and Drug Trafficking

Hans A. von Spakovsky

In the following viewpoint, Hans A. von Spakovsky argues that the DACA program was created in 2012 without legal authority and its termination is long overdue. Several states filed a lawsuit to invalidate and therefore end the program. Von Spakovsky further maintains that to continue DACA is to continue human and drug trafficking to everyone's detriment. Hans A. von Spakovsky is the manager of the Heritage Foundation's Election Law Reform Initiative and a senior legal fellow in Heritage's Meese Center for Legal and Judicial Studies. He is a former Department of Justice attorney.

"DACA Should Be Overturned. A New Lawsuit Might Succeed in Doing That," by Hans A. von Spakovsky, The Heritage Foundation, May 3, 2018. Reprinted by permission.

As you read, consider the following questions:

1. About how many illegal immigrants have been protected by DACA?
2. According to this viewpoint, which states filed a lawsuit claiming President Obama did not have the legal authority to create DACA?
3. What is the DAPA program?

A lawsuit filed Tuesday by Texas and six other states may finally result in the long-overdue termination of the DACA program, which was created without legal authority by President Obama in 2012 to allow children brought into the U.S. illegally to temporarily remain here under certain conditions.

The lawsuit does not address the question of whether allowing the roughly 700,000 illegal immigrants protected from deportation under DACA is a good policy or a bad one. Instead, the suit contends correctly that President Obama exceeded his authority under law and under the Constitution to create DACA without the approval of Congress and without taking other required steps.

Whatever the outcome of the suit, the ruling seems certain to be appealed and wind up in the U.S. Supreme Court.

DACA stands for Deferred Action for Childhood Arrivals. President Trump announced in September that he wanted to phase out the program beginning in March, but federal judges blocked him from doing so after lawsuits were filed to keep DACA in place.

The lawsuit filed Tuesday against the U.S. Department of Homeland Security in U.S. District Court in Brownsville, Texas, correctly says DACA must be invalidated because President Obama had no legal right to create the program "without congressional authorization."

The states contend that if Congress wants to, it has the authority under the Constitution to create whatever program it wants for the illegal immigrants affected by DACA. But the president doesn't have that power acting alone.

This is a critical point. Under the Constitution, the president can't change laws strictly on his own authority just because he thinks such a change is a good idea that will benefit the nation. Congress is a co-equal branch of government and must approve new laws.

If this were not the case, we could have one-person rule by the president—destroying the checks and balances between branches of government that are a key part of the separation of powers in the Constitution and that safeguard our freedom.

The state of Texas was joined by Alabama, Arkansas, Louisiana, Nebraska, South Carolina and West Virginia in filing the lawsuit Tuesday.

In addition to lacking congressional authorization, the seven states say DACA should be thrown out because it:

- Violates federal immigration law.
- Was implemented without the notice-and-comment procedures required for all substantive government regulations and policies under the Administrative Procedure Act.
- Violates the "Take Care" Clause of the Constitution—the provision that requires the president to "take Care that the Laws be faithfully executed."

DACA essentially gives a free pass to illegal immigrants who arrived in the U.S. before turning 16 by June 2007, granting them "lawful presence" with access to a myriad of government benefits, including work authorizations and Social Security benefits.

The lawsuit filed by seven states claims that DACA is just as "contrary to federal law" as the 2014 Deferred Action for Parents of Americans and Lawful Permanent Residents (DAPA) program, also created by President Obama.

The 5th U.S. Circuit Court of Appeals halted DAPA in 2015. That decision was affirmed by a divided Supreme Court when it had just eight justices, following the death of Justice Antonin Scalia.

The DAPA program gave illegal immigrants who were parents of children who were American citizens (usually because the children were born in the U.S.) or whose children were legal permanent residents the same type of amnesty and benefits as the DACA program gave to children brought to the U.S. illegally.

But as the 5th Circuit noted when it stopped the implementation of DAPA, letting a president exercise such power "would allow (the president) to grant lawful presence and work authorization to any illegal alien in the United States—an untenable position in light of the intricate system of immigration classifications and employment eligibility" under federal law.

Texas and the other states involved in the successful lawsuit against DAPA had threatened to amend their lawsuit and add a claim against DACA. But when the Trump administration rescinded DACA—announcing it would not issue or renew DACA permits starting March 5 this year—the states dismissed their DACA lawsuit.

The seven states revived their lawsuit Tuesday to counter the errant injunctions blocking President Trump from ending DACA that were issued by U.S. district courts in California, New York and Washington, D.C.

In January, a California federal judge blocked President Trump's decision to end DACA.

A federal judge in the nation's capital recently issued another decision that the seven states argue "took the remarkable additional step of vacating the executive's decision to wind down DACA, granting summary judgment that the wind-down was substantively unlawful … and ordering the Executive to continue issuing new DACA applications as well," although that judge stayed his order for 90 days.

In addition to all of the legal claims against DACA, the seven states point out that the Obama administration's overall refusal to enforce immigration laws "caused a humanitarian crisis."

The states cite a 2013 federal court decision that said the Obama administration "encouraged international child smuggling across the Texas-Mexico border" because even though the federal government arrested human smugglers, "it completed the criminal conspiracy ... by delivering the minors to the custody" of their parents who were in the country illegally.

By promoting human trafficking, the Obama administration helped "fund the illegal drug cartels which are a very real danger for both citizens of this country and Mexico," the lawsuit filed Tuesday says.

The states want the U.S. District Court to declare the original 2012 DACA program invalid. They also plan to file a motion asking the federal court to issue a preliminary injunction stopping the federal government from issuing or renewing any DACA permits in the future.

The seven states assert that their "lawsuit is emphatically about the rule of law." The "policy merits of immigration laws are debated in and decided by Congress," not the executive branch, which "does not exercise a lawmaking role."

Here's the bottom line:

President Obama had no constitutional or statutory authority to create DACA and provide what amounted to an administrative amnesty program for illegal immigrants.

It is bizarre for judges in California, New York and elsewhere to hold that a president cannot reverse the executive actions of a prior president—particularly when they were improper to start with. It is time the courts recognized that.

> *"[The Trump] administration 'seemed to be saying...if we're going to allow Dreamers to stay in this country, we want a wall.'"*

Dreamers Are Being Treated Like Political Hostages

Luis Gómez Romero

In the following viewpoint, Luis Gómez Romero argues that President Trump's policy to end Deferred Action for Childhood Arrivals (DACA) is a power play move against Mexico to force Mexico to pay for the US-Mexico border wall. Almost 80 percent of the children affected were born in Mexico and are now at risk of deportation. Romero discusses the long history of Mexican immigration into the United States for work. Luis Gómez Romero is a senior lecturer in human rights, constitutional law and legal theory at the University of Wollongong in Australia.

As you read, consider the following questions:

1. What is DACA?
2. What is the Bracero program?
3. What was the 1986 Immigration Reform and Control Act?

Fulfilling one of United States president Donald Trump's campaign promises, US Attorney General Jeff Sessions recently announced the end of the Deferred Action for Childhood Arrivals (DACA) programme. The initiative, launched by former president Barack Obama in 2012, allows people brought to the US illegally as children the temporary right to live, study and work in the country.

DACA protections will begin to expire in six months, giving the US Congress a short window to legislate the now precarious futures of the 787,580 so-called "Dreamers" who currently benefit from the programme.

In Mexico, as in the US, Sessions' announcement was met with distress. Nearly 80% of the programme's recipients were born in Mexico, and ending DACA exposes 618,342 undocumented young Mexicans (as well as 28,371 Salvadorans, 19,792 Guatemalans and 18,262 Hondurans) to deportation. Many in this group, who range in age from 15 to 36, were brought to the US as babies.

There's been some speculation that the US president is using DACA as a bargaining chip. North of the border, commentators think this is about making a deal with Democrats in Congress.

But as a Mexican scholar of US-Mexico political history, I would argue that the DACA decision is more like a power play in Trump's ongoing battle with the government of Mexico. So far President Enrique Peña Nieto has refused the White House's demands that his country pay for the proposed southern border wall. And he only agreed to renegotiate the North American Free Trade Agreement after Trump threatened to withdraw the US from it.

White House Press Secretary Sarah Huckabee Sanders all but confirmed that Trump sees DACA as a political weapon when she acceded to a reporter's assertion that the administration "seemed to be saying…if we're going to allow Dreamers to stay in this country, we want a wall".

White House Press Secretary Sarah Sanders on how DACA relates the proposed US-Mexico border wall.

Either way, I'd contend that Donald Trump is not only holding nearly a million innocent people hostage, trying to exchange dreams for bricks, he's also neglecting the complex history of Mexican migration to the US—a centuries-long tale that, like all national borders, has (at least) two sides.

Where DREAMS Come True

Long before Trump ran for president, American politicians blamed Mexico for not doing enough to keep poor citizens from migrating northward. Mexicans, in turn, tend to blame the US for creating the demand for cheap labour.

The two cross-border problems are deeply intertwined. And because the US and Mexico have both benefited from undocumented migration, each country's efforts to control it have been ambiguous at best.

It is true that Mexico's economy has long been unable to provide enough decent work for its people. Though unemployment has ranged from 3% to 4% for the last two decades, underemployment is deep. In 2016, 14.52% of the Mexican labour force was either working fewer than 35 hours per week or being paid under the meagre daily minimum wage (US$4.50 a day).

For Mexico, then, migration is a safety valve, releasing social tensions that would arise if impoverished migrants stayed home. Mexicans abroad also send large amounts of money to their families in the form of remittances, injecting some US$27 billion into the Mexican economy last year.

Simple economics, however, teach us that demand begets supply. For generations, the modern US economy has thrived on low-wage Mexican labour. Even when nativism surged under president Woodrow Wilson (1913-1921), who signed the Immigration Act of 1917 barring Asian immigration, Congress allowed continued recruitment of Mexicans to til American fields and lay American railroad tracks.

This trend continued throughout the 20th century. In 1942, the US and Mexico jointly instituted the Bracero programme, under which millions of Mexican labourers were hired to work agricultural jobs in the US while many able-bodied American men were off fighting World War II.

While under contract, *braceros* were given housing and paid a minimum wage of thirty cents an hour. By the time the programme ended, in 1964 (nearly two decades after the war's end), the US had sponsored some 5 million border crossings in 24 states.

Workers who came into the US illegally were swiftly incorporated into the Bracero system, too. One of the more bizarre practices in the history of US immigration policy was the so-called "drying out" of "wetbacks", a derogatory official term for undocumented workers.

When the Border Patrol arrested a "wet" worker on a farm, officials would transport him to the border to set foot on Mexican soil—i.e., ritualistically "deport" him—and then allow him to step back into the US, where he would be hired to work legally as a *bracero*.

Mexicans have been crossing the border ever since, hoping to find the steady work and eventual acceptance that the Bracero programme once offered. In the 1965-1986 period, for example, undocumented Mexicans made approximately 27.9 million entries into the US (offset by 23.3 million departures). In that same period approximately 4.6 million established residence in the country.

Without Bracero-style government support, American citizens and firms have simply employed those migrants under the table. Undocumented Mexicans dominate the US agricultural sector, but they are also construction workers, line cooks, landscapers—even Wall Street brokers and journalists.

In 1986, Ronald Reagan signed the Immigration Reform and Control Act, a crackdown that promised tighter security at the Mexican border and strict penalties for employers who hired undocumented workers. However, the bill also offered amnesty to immigrants who had entered the country before 1982.

The term "Dreamers" itself refers to another American attempt at immigration reform, the bipartisan Development, Relief and

Education for Alien Minors (DREAM) Act of 2001, which would have offered permanent legal residency to young people brought to the US as infants.

That bill was never passed. The Obama administration devised the DACA programme as a compromise to protect those young people, many of whom have never known any country but the US.

Bricks for Dreams

Chicana scholar Gloria Anzaldúa once described the border as *"una herida abierta"* —an open wound—where "the Third World grates against the first and bleeds". The Dreamers are children born of this wound.

Their uncertain fate has moved Mexicans, offering president Peña Nieto a rare chance to occupy the moral high ground. His administration has been ridden by successive scandals for months, including very public corruption and illegal espionage on Mexican citizens.

Peña Nieto conveyed his support for DACA recipients in his September 2 State of the Union address, saying:

I send affectionate greetings to the young beneficiaries of the administrative measure that protects those who arrived as infants to the United States. To all of you, young dreamers, our great recognition, admiration and solidarity without reservations.

He later tweeted that any Dreamers deported to Mexico would be welcomed back "with open arms", offering them access to credit, education, scholarships and health services.

In a statement, the Mexican Foreign Ministry acknowledged its northern neighbour's sovereign right to determine its immigration policy but expressed "profound regret" that "thousands of young people" have been thrust into a state of turmoil and fear.

Trump seems willing to use any tactic necessary to get his wall built. If the US Congress does finally agree on a way to protect the Dreamers, it will give these young immigrants the American future they deserve, but no wall—be it Mexican-funded or otherwise— will stop other young Mexicans from trying to build their own.

▌ *"The DREAM Act is a nightmare."*

In-State Tuition Under the DREAM Act Violates Federal Immigration Law

Kris Kobach

In the following viewpoint, Kris Kobach argues against the DREAM Act. The author cautions that the Development, Relief, and Education for Alien Minors (DREAM) Act allows for in-state tuition for illegal immigrants, for violating federal immigration law, and for allowing legal aliens to pay more for tuition than their illegal counterparts. The DREAM Act has been introduced and amended several times since 2001. The most recent iteration is the American Dream and Promise Act of 2019. None of these bills has passed to date. Kris Kobach is a US politician and the secretary of state for Kansas. Formerly, he was chairman of the Republican Party in Kansas.

As you read, consider the following questions:

1. Which ten states offer in-state tuition to illegal immigrants?
2. Why did California governor Gray Davis not sign the in-state illegal alien tuition legislation the first time?
3. Why did Kansas students bring a lawsuit against the federal government?

"The Senate Immigration Bill Rewards Lawbreaking: Why the DREAM Act Is a Nightmare," by Kris Kobach, The Heritage Foundation, August 14, 2006. Reprinted by permission.

It is no secret that the Comprehensive immigration Reform Act of 2006 (S. 2611), passed by the U.S. Senate on May 25, 2006, contains numerous provisions that reward illegal aliens for violating federal immigration law. What is less well known is that the Senate bill also condones the violation of federal law by 10 U.S. states. Indeed, S. 2611 expressly shields these states from liability for their past violations of federal law.

These absurdities are found in the Development, Relief, and Education for Alien Minors (DREAM) Act provisions of S. 2611.[1] Just before the Senate Judiciary Committee approved the first version of the bill in the evening of March 27, 2006, Senator Richard Durbin (D-IL) offered the DREAM Act as an amendment. It passed on a voice vote and was in the compromise version of the bill that the Senate passed in May.

The DREAM Act is a nightmare. It repeals a 1996 federal law that prohibits any state from offering in-state tuition rates to illegal aliens unless the state also offers in-state tuition rates to all U.S. citizens. On top of that, the DREAM Act offers a separate amnesty to illegal-alien students.

The DREAM Act

On its own, the DREAM Act never stood a chance of passing. For years, polls have shown consistently that overwhelming majorities of voters oppose giving in-state tuition benefits to illegal aliens. Not surprisingly, the DREAM Act languished in committee for four years until the opportunity arose to hitch it to the Senate's immigration bill.

Events of the past 10 years illustrate how the DREAM Act would undermine the rule of law. In September 1996, Congress passed the landmark Illegal immigration Reform and Immigrant Responsibility Act (IIRIRA). Led by Lamar Smith (R-TX) in the House of Representatives and Alan Simpson (R-WY) in the Senate, Congress significantly toughened the nation's immigration laws. To his credit, President Bill Clinton signed the bill into law.

Open-borders advocates in some states-most notably California-had already raised the possibility of offering in-state tuition rates to illegal aliens who attend public universities. To prevent such a development, the IIRIRA's sponsors inserted a clearly worded provision that prohibited any state from doing so unless it provided the same discounted tuition to all U.S. citizens:

> Notwithstanding any other provision of law, an alien who is not lawfully present in the United States shall not be eligible on the basis of residence within a State (or a political subdivision) for any postsecondary education benefit unless a citizen or national of the United States is eligible for such a benefit (in no less an amount, duration, and scope) without regard to whether the citizen or national is such a resident.[2]

Members of Congress reasoned that no state would be interested in giving up the extra revenue from out-of-state students, so this provision would ensure that illegal aliens would not be rewarded with a taxpayer-subsidized college education. The IIRIRA's proponents never imagined that some states might simply disobey federal law.

States Subsidizing the College Education of Illegal Aliens

However, that is precisely what happened. In 1999, radical liberals in the California legislature pushed ahead with their plan to have taxpayers subsidize the college education of illegal aliens. Assemblyman Marco Firebaugh (D) sponsored a bill that would have made illegal aliens who had resided in California for three years during high school eligible for in-state tuition at California community colleges and universities.

Democrat Governor Gray Davis vetoed the bill in January 2000, stating clearly in his veto message that it would violate federal law:

> [U]ndocumented aliens are ineligible to receive postsecondary education benefits based on state residence.... IIRIRA would require that all out-of-state Legal residents be eligible for this

same benefit. Based on Fall 1998 enrollment figures...this legislation could result in a revenue loss of over $63.7 million to the state.[3]

Undeterred, Firebaugh introduced his bill again, and the California legislature passed it again. In 2002, facing flagging poll numbers and desperate to rally Hispanic voters to his cause, Governor Davis signed the bill.

Meanwhile, similar interests in Texas succeeded in enacting their own version of the bill. Over the next four years, interest groups lobbying for illegal aliens introduced similar legislation in most of the other states.

The majority of state legislatures had the good sense to reject the idea, but eight states followed the examples of California and Texas, including some states in the heart of "red" America. Today, the 10 states that offer in-state tuition to illegal aliens are California, Illinois, Kansas, Nebraska, New Mexico, New York, Oklahoma, Texas, Utah, and Washington.

In most of these states, the law was passed under cover of darkness because public opinion was strongly against subsidizing the college education of illegal aliens at taxpayer expense. The governors even declined to hold press conferences or signing ceremonies heralding the new laws.

However, in Nebraska, the last of the 10 states to pass the law, something unusual happened. During the 2006 session, Nebraska's unicameral legislature passed an in-state tuition bill for illegal aliens. Governor Dave Heineman vetoed the bill because it violated federal law and was bad policy. In mid-April, the legislature, which included 20 lame-duck Senators, overrode his veto by a vote of 30 to 19.

The veto would become an issue in the 2006 Republican gubernatorial primary. Heineman's opponent was the legendary University of Nebraska football coach and sitting U.S. Representative Tom Osborne, a political demigod in the Cornhusker State. Osborne had never received less than 82 percent of the vote in any election. Heineman, on the other hand, had not yet won a gubernatorial election. He became governor in 2005 when Governor Mike Johanns resigned to become U.S. Secretary of Agriculture.

Few believed that Heineman had a chance of winning the primary, but Coach Osborne fumbled. He criticized Heineman for vetoing the in-state tuition bill and indicated that he favored the idea of giving subsidized tuition to illegal aliens. The voters reacted negatively, and Heineman surged ahead in the final weeks to beat Osborn by 50 percent to 44 percent in the primary election on May 9, 2006. After the vote, both candidates said the tuition issue had been decisive.

State-Subsidized Lawbreaking

In all 10 states, the in-state tuition laws make for shockingly bad policy.

First, providing in-state tuition rates to illegal aliens amounts to giving them a taxpayer-financed education. In contrast, out-of-state students pay the full cost of their education. This gift to illegal aliens costs taxpayers a great deal of money at a time when tuition rates are rising across the country. The costs of these subsidies are staggering. For example, California taxpayers pay more than $50 million annually to subsidize the college education of thousands of illegal aliens.

Second, these states are encouraging aliens to violate federal immigration law. Indeed, breaking federal law is a prerequisite for illegal aliens because state laws expressly deny in-state tuition to Legal aliens who have valid student visas. An alien is eligible for in-state tuition only if he remains in the state in violation of federal law and evades federal law enforcement. Legal aliens must pay out-of-state tuition. The states are directly rewarding this illegal behavior.

This situation is comparable to a state passing a law that rewards residents with state tax credits for cheating on their federal income taxes. These 10 states are providing direct financial subsidies to those who violate federal law.

Third, not only are such laws unfair to aliens who follow the law, but they are slaps in the faces of law-abiding American citizens. For example, a student from Missouri who attends Kansas University and has always played by the rules and obeyed the law is charged three times the tuition charged to an alien whose very presence in the country is a violation of federal criminal law.

Even if a good argument could be made for giving in-state tuition benefits to illegal aliens, the bottom line is that the policy violates federal law. These 10 states have brazenly cast aside the constraints imposed by Congress and the U.S. Constitution.

Pending Lawsuits

In July 2004, a group of U.S. citizen students from out of state filed suit in federal district court in Kansas to enjoin the state from providing in-state tuition rates to illegal aliens.[4] They pointed out that Kansas is clearly violating federal law and the Equal Protection Clause of the U.S. Constitution by discriminating against them in favor of illegal aliens.

The district judge did not render any decision on the central questions of the case. Instead, he avoided the issues entirely by issuing a particularly weak ruling that the plaintiffs lacked a private right of action to bring their statutory challenge and lacked standing to bring their Equal Protection challenge. The case is currently before the U.S. Court of Appeals for the Tenth Circuit. Regrettably, the wheels of justice grind slowly, and a decision is unlikely before the spring of 2007.

Meanwhile, in December 2005, another group of U.S. citizen students filed a class-action suit in a California state court.[5] They too maintain that the state is violating federal law and the U.S. Constitution. Pursuant to a California civil rights statute, they are also seeking damages to compensate them for the extra tuition that they have paid above that charged to illegal aliens. Additional suits will likely be filed by U.S. citizens in the eight other states.

Another Senate Bill Amnesty

Just when it looked as if U.S. citizens might vindicate their rights under federal law and the wayward states would be held accountable, the Senate passed the immigration bill, offering the offending states a pardon.

The DREAM Act provisions, which are buried more than 600 pages into S. 2611, grant an unusual reprieve to the offending states. They retroactively repeal the 1996 federal law that the 10 states violated, making it as though the provisions in the 1996 law never existed.[6]

On top of this insult to the rule of law, the DREAM Act would create a massive independent amnesty in addition to the even larger amnesty that the rest of S. 2611 would confer. This amnesty opens a wide path to citizenship for any alien who entered the country before the age of 16 and has been in the country for at least five years. As with the rest of the Senate bill, the guiding notion seems to be "The longer you have violated federal law, the better."

Beyond that, all the alien needs is a high school diploma or a GED earned in the United States. Alternatively, he need only persuade an institution of higher education in the United States-any community college, technical school, or college-to admit him.

The DREAM Act abandons any pretense of "temporary status" for the illegal aliens who apply. Instead, all amnesty recipients are awarded lawful permanent resident (green card) status. The only caveat is that the alien's status is considered "conditional" for the first six years. To move on to the normal green card, the alien need only obtain a degree from any institution of higher education, complete two years toward a bachelor's degree, or show that doing so would present a hardship to himself or his family members. Of course, an alien with a normal green card can bring in family members and seek citizenship.

Furthermore, the DREAM Act makes it absurdly easy for just about any illegal alien-even one who does not qualify for the amnesty-to evade the law. According to Section 624(f), once an alien files an application-any application, no matter how ridiculous-the federal government is prohibited from deporting him. Moreover, with few exceptions, federal officers are prohibited from either using information from the application to deport the alien or sharing that information with another federal agency, under threat of up to $10,000 fine.

Thus, an alien's admission that he has violated federal immigration law cannot be used against him-even if he never had any chance of qualifying for the DREAM Act amnesty in the first place. The DREAM Act also makes illegal aliens eligible for various federal student loans and work-study programs.

Conclusion

In addition to being a dream for those who have broken the law, the DREAM Act raises an even larger issue regarding the relationship between states and the federal government. The 10 states have created a 21st century version of the nullification movement-defying federal law simply because they do not like it. In so doing, they have challenged the basic structure of the republic. The DREAM Act would pardon this offense and, in so doing, encourage states to defy other federal law in the future.

One thing that has been learned in the struggle to enforce federal immigration laws is that states cannot be allowed to undermine the federal efforts to enforce them. Rule of law can be fully restored only if all levels of government are working to uphold it.

Notes

1. S. 2611, § 621-632.
2. 8 U.S. Code, § 1623.
3. Gray Davis, veto message to California Assembly on AB 1197, September 29, 2000, at info.sen.ca.gov/pub/99-00/bill/asm/ ab_1151-1200/ab_1197_vt_20000929.html (August 10, 2006).
4. See Day v. Sebelius, 376 F. Supp. 2d 1022 (2005).
5. See Stuart Silverstein, "Out-of-State Students Sue over Tuition: Plaintiffs Are Challenging California Practices That Require Them to Pay Higher College Costs Than Some Illegal Immigrants," Los Angeles Times, December 15, 2005, p. B3
6. S. 2611, § 623.

> *"This is exactly the sort of action the law itself regards as morally inappropriate."*

Protect the Dreamers, Protect the Law

Michael Blake

In the following viewpoint, Michael Blake argues that the federal government's plan to end Deferred Action for Childhood Arrivals (DACA) program does not take into account that these immigrants who entered illegally did so as children. They are, therefore, not to be prosecuted as adults and to do so would be morally irresponsible. Children who illegally crossed the border have the US Constitutional right to attend public school. The fact that this children reside within the United States gives them rights that must not be taken away. Michael Blake is professor of philosophy, public policy, and governance at the University of Washington.

As you read, consider the following questions:

1. What was Attorney General Jeff Sessions' argument?
2. According to this viewpoint, why is deportation not a punishment?
3. Why are these DACA immigrants not like other people?

"Why Deporting the 'Dreamers' Is Immoral," by Michael Blake, The Conversation, 08/28/2018. https://theconversation.com/why-deporting-the-dreamers-is-immoral-91738. Licensed under CC BY 4.0.

On Feb. 26, the U.S. Supreme Court refused to review a federal judge's order that the Trump administration continue the Deferred Action for Childhood Arrivals program.

It was back in September 2017 that President Donald Trump and Attorney General Jeff Sessions announced the end of the Obama-era program that shields hundreds of thousands of undocumented immigrants brought to the United States as children. Sessions argued that this program rewarded those who disobeyed the laws of the United States. The United States has an obligation to "end the lawlessness" of DACA, he argued, by winding down the program and, at the same time, making a case for the deportation of the "Dreamers" or those previously protected by DACA.

For now, the Supreme Court's refusal to hear the case leaves the program in place.

As a scholar, who has tried to understand how morality should be applied to politics and law, I do not agree with Sessions.

Respect for the law entails respect for moral values. Protecting the Dreamers isn't about rejecting the rule of law. Rather, it reflects respect for the morality that the law proclaims.

Can Children Be Held Morally Responsible?

The people covered by DACA came to the United States when they were children. Even if their entry into the United States was unlawful, the violation was committed by a child. The law of the United States affirms the common sense thought that children are unlike adults in the degree to which they morally responsible.

The laws of the United States do not, for example, let children create binding contracts. Children are not allowed to perform many actions open to adults: They cannot smoke tobacco, get tattoos, drink alcohol, drive automobiles, nor vote in federal elections. Nor are they liable to the same sorts of criminal punishments as adults.

Their degree of culpability for criminal acts is generally taken to be lower than that of adults—and some punishments, such as the death penalty, are taken off the table for children entirely.

Any Immigrant Can Seek Asylum by Law

President Donald Trump announced a plan today to block asylum seekers who enter the country between ports of entry and to massively expand detention in tent cities for all individuals seeking asylum, including children. He promised a "comprehensive" executive order next week.

The following statement is from Beth Werlin, executive director of the American Immigration Council:

> The United States has long stood as a beacon of hope for individuals seeking safety. Our asylum laws and practices must continue to reflect this. Locking up thousands of asylum-seeking parents and children in 'massive tent cities' does not make America safer.
>
> Through our work on the Dilley Pro Bono Project, we know that family detention traumatizes children and limits access to attorneys. There are proven alternatives to detention in use by the government and studies show that 96 percent of released families who applied for asylum attend their immigration court hearings.
>
> The law is clear and unambiguous. Any person inside the United States, regardless how he or she entered, may apply for asylum. Today's announcement is a dangerous political stunt which takes a vital lifeline away from individuals fleeing violence and persecution in their home countries. Our asylum system is strong enough to handle the arrival of families fleeing horrific conditions without compromising our national security.

"American Immigration Council Condemns President Trump's Plan to Block and Detain Asylum Seekers," American Immigration Council, November 1, 2018.

In the case of DACA, however, deporting the Dreamers would involve subjecting people to a significant punishment. And it would do so in response to an action people took when they were children. This is exactly the sort of action the law itself regards as morally inappropriate.

Punishment and Deportation

One response to this argument against deportation might be to say that deportation is not, in fact, a punishment. It is simply refusing to provide a benefit - namely, the right to remain within the United States. The foreign citizen who is refused the right to migrate to the United States is inconvenienced – but that's hardly the same as being punished. And, indeed, deportation is generally understood in law to be a "civil penalty," rather than a punishment.

Even a civil penalty, though, is something whose imposition must be justified morally. The justices of the Supreme Court of the United States have sometimes emphasized that being expelled from one's home involves the destruction of much of what one values. It is the destruction of all that one has built.

This fact was recognized early in the history of the American legal system. Founding father James Madison, in discussing the Alien and Sedition Acts of 1798, argued strongly against deportation. He said:

> "... if a banishment of this sort, be not a punishment, and among the severest of punishments, it will be difficult to imagine a doom to which the name might be applied."

The Supreme Court agrees. It recently reaffirmed its commitment to the thought that deportation, even if a mere penalty, is "a uniquely severe" one.

Residency and Rights

The DACA opponent might, in reply, argue that the morality of the law applies only to those people who are legitimately subject to the law. The laws of the United States might insist, in other words, that the United States has no particular obligations to those people who have entered into the political community, defined by its jurisdictional limits, without any right.

Here, too, the law of the United States disagrees.

The mere fact of being found within the United States—whether rightfully or not—provides one with significant rights under the

Constitution. The law itself gives the undocumented legal rights to bring claims in vindication of their constitutional rights.

Undocumented children, for instance, have a constitutional right to be provided with public schooling. The Supreme Court, in defending this principle, argued that all people within the state's jurisdiction—"even aliens whose presence in this country is unlawful"—are guaranteed due process under the law.

Morality and Migration

Yes, nothing in the law requires the opening of all borders. And it is true that the United States does not have an obligation to provide the right to enter or stay in the country to all who might desire that right.

However, the Dreamers are not like other people. The simple fact of where they are now provides them with constitutional standing denied to outsiders.

And, as emphasized earlier, whatever wrong they might have done in crossing into the United States, they did as children. The revocation of DACA, however, would announce that they are rightly subjected to a significant—indeed, a devastating—punishment, in virtue of an act committed in childhood.

Law is not the same as morality. But morality can sometimes look to law, in determining where its deliberations might begin. If the deportation of the DACA recipients would violate the moral principles that underlie the American legal system, there is at least some reason to think that such deportation is morally wrong.

Contrary to Jeff Sessions, I believe that the United States would not respect the law best by deporting the Dreamers. It would respect it best by living up to the moral ideals that make the law worth following.

> *"Providing amnesty and potential citizenship to DACA recipients and other illegal immigrants before we have a secure border will only encourage even more illegal immigration."*

It's Time to End DACA

Hans A. von Spakovsky

In the following viewpoint, Hans von Spakovsky argues that at the crux of the debate whether to extend or expire DACA, the system our founding fathers set up for checks and balances should be put into action. Congress needs to approve presidential actions; the president should not sidestep Congress by issuing executive orders. Hans A. von Spakovsky is the manager of the Heritage Foundation's Election Law Reform Initiative and a senior legal fellow in Heritage's Meese Center for Legal and Judicial Studies. He is a former department of justice attorney.

As you read, consider the following questions:

1. What is the argument in favor of DACA?
2. What is the purpose of checks and balances?
3. According to this viewpoint, what percentage of DACA beneficiaries have only achieved a high school education?

"It's Time to End DACA—It's Unconstitutional Unless Approved by Congress," by Hans A. von Spakovsky, The Heritage Foundation, January 25, 2019. Reprinted by permission.

It's disappointing that the Supreme Court failed Tuesday to grant the Trump administration's appeal of a lower court order that prevents the president from ending the Deferred Action for Childhood Arrivals (DACA) program. But it's not the end of the story.

Importantly, the high court didn't reject the request filed by the Justice Department to allow President Trump to end DACA. The request is still pending.

If the Supreme Court grants the Justice Department's appeal of the lower court order between now and the end of June, the case to determine the fate of the DACA program will be heard during the next term of the court that begins in October.

Roughly 700,000 immigrants brought to the U.S. illegally as children are protected from deportation by DACA. The argument in favor of the program is that the children didn't choose to break the law and so should not be punished because their parents violated immigration laws by bringing them to the U.S.

But the central issue at stake in the DACA case is not whether the young people now protected by DACA deserve or don't deserve to be allowed to stay in the U.S. The issue at stake is what power the Constitution gives the president to act alone by issuing executive orders, without seeking approval from Congress.

The framers of the Constitution very deliberately set up a system of government where power was divided between the president and Congress, with the courts given the power to rule on disputes. These checks and balances were created to prevent one person from ruling the country as an all-powerful king or dictator. The system has worked brilliantly.

To preserve that system of checks and balances, the Supreme Court should hear the appeal of the lower court case on DACA and give President Trump the authority to end the program.

No matter what view you may have about whether the DACA program is good public policy, the decision to extend amnesty and government benefits to illegal immigrants is a decision that under the Constitution can only be made by Congress—not the president.

President Trump announced Saturday that he would support legislation in Congress to extend DACA protections for three years for the 700,000 young people now in the program, and also support a three-year extension of another program that allows 300,000 immigrants from countries stricken by disasters or conflicts to stay in the U.S. But in return, the president said Congress would need to approve the $5.7 billion he has requested for a barrier along portions of our southern border.

Rather than agree to the president's compromise proposal that would give DACA the congressional approval it needs to pass constitutional muster for three more years, Democratic leaders in the House and Senate rejected the offer immediately because they refuse to fund the expansion of current border fencing.

DACA was created by an executive order issued by President Obama in 2012 without the approval of Congress – despite the fact that Article I, Section 8 of the Constitution assigns complete authority to Congress to determine our nation's immigration rules.

DACA provided a temporary promise that the government wouldn't deport immigrants who were younger than 16 when they were brought to the U.S. illegally. DACA also provided these illegal immigrants with government benefits, such as work authorizations. And it allowed the president to defer deporting these illegal immigrants for years.

But providing administrative amnesty and access to government benefits is beyond a president's constitutional and statutory authority. This was the ruling of the 5th U.S. Circuit Court of Appeals when it upheld a court order against President Obama's attempt to expand DACA and implement another program with similar benefits in 2014, called Deferred Action for Parents of Americans and Lawful Permanent Residents (DAPA).

The appellate court said that federal immigration law "flatly does not permit the reclassification of millions of illegal aliens as lawfully present and thereby make them newly eligible for a host of federal and state benefits, including work authorizations." A

THE DEPARTMENT OF HOMELAND SECURITY HAS TO EXPLAIN WHY IT IS OVERTURNING DACA

In a Twitter message, de Blasio praised the court ruling, adding that the authorities were ready to help DACA recipients living in New York City.

Former US President Barack Obama established DACA by an executive order issued in 2012. The program grants temporary work and residency privileges to undocumented immigrants—known as "Dreamers"—who arrived illegally in the United States as children.

President Donald Trump's administration announced in September that it would end DACA on March 5.

But according to documents filed in the US District Court for the District of Columbia late Tuesday night, Judge John Bates ruled that the Department of Homeland Security (DHS), which administers the program, did not explain why it ended DACA, Sputnik reported.

"Neither the meager legal reasoning nor the assessment of litigation risk provided by DHS to support its rescission decision is sufficient to sustain termination of the DACA program," the ruling said.

The judge gave DHS 90 days to better explain its decision to overturn DACA, otherwise the program will be allowed to continue, and the federal government will be forced to resume accepting new applications.

**"US Judge's Order to Resume DACA Program 'Victory for Justice': NYC Mayor,"
Tasnim News Agency, April 25, 2018.**

divided U.S. Supreme Court upheld this decision in 2016, leaving the court order against DAPA in place.

The Trump administration announced in 2017 that—given the Supreme Court's ruling in the DAPA case—it was going to wind DACA down, too, since the same arguments accepted by the courts as to the unlawfulness of President Obama's actions on DAPA applied equally to DACA. This is a logical and obvious conclusion.

President Trump said the wind-down would not immediately terminate the two-year grants of immunity that DACA recipients had received. This would give Congress time to act if it believed the DACA program was something that should be authorized through federal immigration law.

Given the huge battle currently going on over immigration policy, funding for a border barrier and the partial government shutdown, it should come as no surprise that Congress did not act on DACA.

Instead, a number of challengers—including the University of California—went to court and managed to convince a federal district court judge and a panel of the 9th U.S. Circuit Court of Appeals to issue a court order preventing the Trump administration from ending DACA.

The lower court rulings defy not only common sense, but the Constitution.

It is untenable to claim that a subsequent president cannot end a program put in place by a prior president—particularly when courts have already held that prior executive action by a president on virtually the same issue was beyond his executive authority, violating the Constitution and statutory law.

No one questions that Congress could implement a DACA- or DAPA-type program. Congress can grant citizenship or amnesty to any immigrants it wants. But a president lacks the authority to do so.

The wisdom of the policy of allowing DACA recipients to spend the rest of their lives in the U.S. and eventually become citizens – as many Democrats in Congress advocate – is also questionable.

The media portrayal of DACA beneficiaries paints a uniformly rosy picture of highly educated, fluent individuals. But that is not in accord with the facts.

For example, according to the most recent figures only 49 percent of DACA beneficiaries have attained a high school education—despite a majority of them now being adults.

Almost no background checks were conducted by the Department of Homeland Security, resulting in illegal immigrants with criminal backgrounds being accepted into the DACA program, including members of the MS-13 criminal gang.

And one study estimates that perhaps as many as a quarter of DACA-eligible illegal immigrants are functionally illiterate in English, while another 46 percent have only "basic" English ability.

Providing amnesty and potential citizenship to DACA recipients and other illegal immigrants before we have a secure border will only encourage even more illegal immigration, just as the 1986 amnesty in the Immigration Reform and Control Act did.

That law provided citizenship to almost 3 million illegal immigrants and was supposed to solve the problem of illegal immigration. Yet within 10 years, there were another almost 6 million illegal immigrants in the U.S.

The federal government should be concentrating on enhancing immigration enforcement and border security to stem the flow of illegal immigrants into the country and reduce the number of them already in the interior of the U.S.

Until we achieve those goals, it is premature to consider any kind of benefits for any immigrants in the U.S. illegally.

The Supreme Court has a duty to take up the Trump administration's DACA appeal and throw out actions by lower courts that are not in accord with the Constitution and federal immigration law. That action would send this issue of whether the DACA program should exist back to where it belongs – not to the president, as President Obama mistakenly believed, but to Congress.

> *"The Residents' Bill of Rights wouldn't increase at all the number of people enjoying a definite legal right of residence, much less a path to citizenship. But it would ensure that all those residing in the United States would be treated a little more justly."*

A Resident's Bill of Rights Would Fix Immigration While Protecting Communities

Nathan Smith

In the following viewpoint Nathan Smith argues for a human rights approach to immigration in the United States. The author is a proponent for open borders, but he freely admits that there is no hope of achieving open borders in the current political climate. The next best thing, he contends, is what he proposes as "The Human Rights and Growth Act." This is a multi-pronged, sustainable solution to many of the country's immigration-related problems. Nathan Smith is an assistant professor of economics at Fresno Pacific University.

As you read, consider the following questions:

1. Why does creating a pathway to citizenship for Dreamers raise as many problems as it solves, according to the viewpoint?
2. What document's language does the author's proposed Resident's Bill of Rights borrow?
3. What does the author mean when he says his proposal is "highly federalist?"

My fundamental convictions have not changed: I support open borders. And yet one can't tilt at windmills too long without feeling a sense of futility and even foolishness. We may have had an impact. We have been noticed in high places, a little. But of course there is no prospect of open borders being adopted as official policy in any of the world's developed countries anytime soon. Meanwhile, there is room for reasonable hope that immigration policy will move quite a ways in the right direction, and for reasonable fear that it will move far in the wrong direction, in the coming years, and it's far from clear that advocating open borders is the best way to help accomplish the former, or avoid the latter. To advocate open borders, assuming, as seems likely, that that aim cannot be achieved for decades at least, can only help indirectly, e.g., by expanding the "Overton window," and might plausibly hurt, by provoking a restrictionist reaction against an open-borders bogeyman. For those idealists who really want to know what justice demands, we've explained that. I'd be happy to explain it again, debate it, whatever. But the value of refining the case for open borders still further seems doubtful until there's evidence that people exist who really want to do the right thing, have read what has been argued so far, and are still unconvinced. My impression is that among people with a thorough exposure to the public case for open borders, as it has been made here and elsewhere, the insufficiency of the arguments offered is not a very important factor in any failure to persuade. Some of the unconvinced just aren't very smart, while more aren't good enough to do the right thing when they start to see it, so they bluster and stonewall and scoff.

So in this post, I'm going to attempt something a bit different, involving an unaccustomed degree of compromise. I'm going to lay out a policy platform that, while falling well short of open borders, lies, I think, at the radical end of what might actually find a coalition to carry it through to success in the United States in the near future. It doesn't institute open borders. If passed, deportations would still occur, and billions who would benefit from immigrating would be excluded from the territory of the United States permanently from birth. Indeed, the centerpiece of this proposed policy, the Residents' Bill of Rights, wouldn't increase at all the number of people enjoying a definite legal right of residence, much less a path to citizenship. But it would ensure that all those residing in the United States would be treated a little more justly. It would make it harder to backslide into a harsh enforcement regime or a reduction of immigrant numbers. It would give the foreign born, however they got there, a certain dignity and a certain security. It would cause many acts of wickedness, many violations of fundamental human rights, to cease. It would give conscientious Americans the right to be substantially less ashamed of the way their government treats immigrants. At the same time, by empowering immigration skeptics to act locally instead of nationally, it would appease some of their more legitimate fears. It would not institute open borders, but I believe it would help to prepare the way.

The coalition I'm envisioning, to whom I think this might appeal and who might carry it through, would include most liberal Democrats, especially those of a commercial and globalist stripe, and many Christian and/or libertarian NeverTrumpers like myself, who in some sense identify, even rather strongly, with conservatives and the GOP, though the Trump era has left us politically homeless. My starting point in designing it is the extreme popularity of the never-passed DREAM Act. The Dreamers, born abroad but raised in America and having no other home, and clearly enjoying a right to stay in America if right and wrong mean anything at all, have become the archetypal immigrants threatened with deportation. But of course, the DREAM Act is a one-time fix. A decade after its passage, unless perfect enforcement magically appears, there would be more similarly situated individuals, born abroad but raised in America and knowing no other home, the deportation of whom should be intolerable to anyone who has a ghost of a conscience. So suppose the Democrats win a surprise supermajority in November 2018 on a pro-DREAM Act platform, and want to use their mandate, not just for a one-time fix, but for a permanent correction of the bad laws that have created the sad plight of the Dreamers, while meanwhile boosting the economy. What might they do?

I would propose the following. It might be called "the Human Rights and Growth Act."

First, remove the cap on H1-Bs. So far, so obvious. Skilled workers contribute to the competitiveness of US-based companies, don't compete for jobs with the most struggling Americans, and aren't a fiscal drain. An arbitrary cap makes no sense. This doesn't particularly help now or future Dreamers, but it's a good way to signal an end to Trumpism and the scapegoating of immigrants even at the cost of sabotaging the economy. All immigrants could sleep a little better feeling that we're making some attempt to make immigration policy rational.

Second, a pathway to citizenship for the Dreamers, because that's what the Dreamers have been led to expect, and what the public wants, and it's the surest way to protect them from deportation, which some unworthy Americans still darkly desire for them. Yet it raises as many problems as it solves. Dreamers are a minority of the undocumented immigrant population. The Dreamer population must be defined somehow. There must be lines drawn, rather arbitrarily, defining who's in and who's out. Good Dreamers, turned citizens, will seek to protect their parents from deportation, as they should. And the more politicians defend the fundamental justice of turning the Dreamers into citizens, the more they'll fuel the case for the next generation of Dreamers to get their citizenship, too. Anticipating this, more undocumented immigrants will come, slipping through the Rio Grande or the Gulf of Mexico, or coming from China in shipping containers, and that's great, but what happens next? Within a few years of the great moral triumph of the DREAM Act, US officials will again find themselves tasked with executing orders to deport people raised in the U.S. from childhood, which everyone now knows, thanks to the DREAM Act debate, is morally wrong. Who'll be the last to get deported for a mistake?

So this brings me to the third plank of my proposal, the most original and doubtless the heaviest political lift. Call it a Residents' Bill of Rights. This gets to the heart of the ethical and constitutional crisis that the Dreamers have brought to a head. I'll first try to frame it in quasi-legislative language, then explain my rationale somewhat, and how I would expect its implementation in law and society to play out.

Residents' Bill of Rights

1. No resident of the United States, defined as anyone living and making their home on US territory, regardless of their legal status, being over 25 years of age, not having been convicted of a violent or property crime and not constituting a demonstrable threat to the public safety, shall be deported to a country where they lack a substantial history of residence. A substantial history of residence shall be defined as three or more years living in a country at an age of 16 years or more, within the twenty years previous to the date of the proposed deportation. Citizenship of a foreign country shall be presumptive evidence of a substantial history of residence there, but if a potential deportee denies that they have a substantial history of residence in their country of citizenship, they shall be given due opportunity to prove otherwise.

2. No resident of the United States living in close proximity, defined as 50 miles or less, to a close relative, defined

as a spouse, parent, child, or sibling, not having been convicted of a violent or property crime and not constituting a demonstrable threat to the public safety, shall be forcibly separated from this family member through deportation without this family member's consent, regardless of whether the family member is a citizen or legal resident of the United States.

3. No person shall be deported, or otherwise required by the laws of the United States to go, to a country where they face a serious threat of violence on account of their religion due to the policies of the government of that country.

4. States and municipal communities shall enjoy a right to offer sanctuary to residents of the United States otherwise legally vulnerable to deportation. No person, therefore, shall be deported without the explicit consent of all state and local governments enjoying jurisdiction at the point where the person was apprehended for deportation.

5. No citizen of the United States shall be deprived of his or her livelihood through the deportation of a foreigner without his or her consent, unless at least two years of advance notice are provided. If a deportation process is initiated, citizens of the United States whose livelihoods are adversely impacted by the deportation shall have four months in which to object, and having done so, four further months in which to prove that their power to earn a livelihood is grievously injured by the proposed deportation. If they prove this successfully, the deportation order shall be suspended for two years subsequent to that determination.

6. No city, town, village, or other legally constituted municipal community, enjoying a coherent democratic government and continuously settled geography, as defined under state law, shall be required to permit the new entry of residents who are not US citizens. Municipal

communities shall be empowered to regulate residency so as to confirm proof of citizenship, so as to exclude non-citizens in general or in particular, before authorizing the purchase or lease of real estate. This right shall not be construed to include the right to expel non-citizens who have already established residency by means that were legal at the time, or to exclude the close family members, defined as spouses, siblings, parents, and children, of legal residents, provided they live in the same dwelling as those residents.

7. National origin shall be a permissible basis for citizens, companies, religious and educational institutions, private voluntary organizations of all sorts, and state, local, and federal governmental entities to decide whom to hire and at what wages, whom to fire or lay off and for what causes, whom to lease or sell real estate and movable goods to and at what prices and rents, and whom to provide services to and at what price, provided that such discrimination is not applied to the direct disadvantage of citizens of the United States.

8. National origin shall be a permissible basis for state and local governments to decide how much tax is owed by a person, provided that no citizen of the United States is required to pay more tax than a similarly situated non-citizen would be.

9. No state or municipal community shall be required to finance or administer welfare or public assistance to residents who lack US citizenship. Instead, they may, if they choose, require beneficiaries to provide proof of citizenship before assistance is provided. They may also provide welfare and public assistance to some non-citizens, on the basis of nationality, education, profession, language, length of residency, or any other criterion they shall see fit to apply, and not to others.

10. All residents of the United States shall enjoy the
    right to work for a single willing employer for up to
    $600 of earnings in a calendar year without providing
    documentation, and for up to $30,000 if the employer
    pays a tax equal to one-third of the worker's wages to
    the federal government, plus any state and local taxes
    that may be levied on this anonymous income. Citizens
    of the United States shall be exempt from reporting
    anonymously earned income for purposes of taxation
    or benefit eligibility determination, but non-citizens
    shall be required to report such income and pay taxes as
    required by any applicable federal, state, and local income
    tax codes.

Obviously, the "bill of rights" language echoes, and the hope
is that the Residents' Bill of Rights could borrow the popularity
of, the original Bill of Rights in the US Constitution.

The first five provisions curtail the right of deportation, and
would introduce an element of human rights and due process into
the immigration enforcement regime which is desperately deficient
today. They would recognize that there are large classes of persons
resident on US territory whom the government cannot justly
remove, and give these persons legal protection. Notably, they don't
quite actually, positively, grant anyone a right to reside in the United
States, much less a path to citizenship. But by greatly reducing the
fear of deportation in which undocumented immigrants live, they
could be expected to grow the stock of immigrants in the United
States. More would overstay visas or slip through the border if
immigration enforcement were less scary, and new undocumented
immigration would be offset by fewer deportations. Provision (10)
would also be an important incentive to immigrate, for people
to whom $30,000 per year in legal, anonymous income might be
very appealing.

Provisions (6)-(9) would, I expect, feel like "concessions" to
many supporters of immigration. But they do something important,
namely, empower individuals, companies, and communities to

protect themselves against the consequences of mass immigration, which I think will continue to be mainly good, but which it's certainly not crazy to fear may be bad in some respects. For those who fear "forced integration" with immigrants due to the operation of anti-discrimination laws, provision (7) ensures that they can "hire American" if they want to. For those who fear that immigrants will be a fiscal drain, provisions (8) and (9) serve as strong protections at least at the state and local levels. Provision (6) is the most offensive to libertarian sensibilities. Yet it's plausible that subtle externalities operate at the neighborhood level, and certainly, until the education system is comprehensively voucherized, most people will have good reason to worry about certain kinds of immigrant children lowering the quality of the schools. I argued in Principles of a Free Society that gated communities are just, provided that the community's use of its streets involves activities that contribute substantially to the flourishing of its members in ways that depend on the peculiar character of the community and its membership. In effect, provision (6) lets towns convert themselves into gated communities. I suspect most of them don't really have a sufficiently rich and shared communal street life that it would really be just for them to exclude immigrants so as to protect it, but it would be far less, if at all, unjust for towns to practice such exclusion, than for the entire country to so so.

The Human Rights and Growth Act wouldn't be easy to pass, of course. It gores sacred cows on both right and left. The right could see it, with good reason, as an assault on national sovereignty and "border security" (in the peculiar sense of that phrase, divorced from its legitimate meaning of securing the border against armed invasion, in which the nativist right likes to use it; note that in this sense the 19th-century United States never enjoyed or aspired to such "border security"). The left could see it as an insidiously undermining equal rights and the social safety net, and introducing into American society a deliberate element of apartheid and class stratification. Yet each side would also get something beyond its wildest dreams. Right-wing communitarians worried about immigrants' impact on the culture could create homogeneous citizenist enclaves where immigrants are excluded, and see how they work. High-minded leftists could celebrate a drastic curtailment of deportation, and exercise their right to create sanctuaries through their local governments.

It's a highly federalist proposal, which empowers state and local governments to make their own immigration policies, shifting in either direction. They could deny immigrants welfare or even exclude then from residing in certain cities and towns (a "right-wing" policy), or grant sanctuary and full welfare benefits (a "left-wing" policy), or they could protect them from deportation while denying them welfare (a "libertarian" policy). Finally, they could, and I think many soon would, maximize locals' prosperity, by banning deportation and immigrant welfare and charging immigrants extra taxes to finance state and local government. House and apartment hunting for immigrants would become a bit more complex, since they'd need to look up residency restrictions in any community they considered moving to. For some, long commutes would be the price of living in America and working in a restrictionist town. But for most, this would be a small price to pay in order to enjoy a lot of new options for avoiding deportation.

Even if it didn't pass now, the strange staying power of the DREAM Act in public discourse shows how even a failed law can become a legitimizing force and a standard of justice. I can imagine a generation waiting in growing indignation until the Human Rights and Growth Act finally gets passed. So, is it a good idea? Who's with me?

Periodical and Internet Sources Bibliography

The following articles have been selected to supplement the diverse views presented in this chapter.

Adam Edelman, "Trump Ends DACA Program, No New Applications Accepted," NBC News, September 5, 2017. www.nbcnews.com/politics/immigration/trump-dreamers-daca-immigration-announcement-n798686

Majority Leader Steny Hoyer, "A Look at H.R. 6, the Dream and Promise Act of 2019, Majorityleader.gov, March 12, 2019. www.majorityleader.gov/content/look-hr6-dream-and-promise-act-2019

Amber Jamieson, "Trump Is Now Using DREAMers As a Bargaining Chip to Get Wall Funding and End the Shutdown," BuzzFeed News, January 19, 2019. www.buzzfeednews.com/article/amberjamieson/trump-immigration-deal-shutdown-daca-dreamers-tps.

Gabe Ortiz, "DACA Recipient Tells Sen. Gillibrand She Fears Being Deported 'to a Country That I Barely Know," Daily Kos, April 10, 2019. www.dailykos.com/stories/2019/4/10/1849260/-DACA-recipient-tells-Sen-Gillibrand-she-fears-being-deported-to-a-country-that-I-barely-know.

Christian Penichet-Paul, "Dream Act of 2019: Bill Summary," National Immigration Forum, March 28, 2019. immigrationforum.org/article/dream-act-of-2019-bill-summary/.

Steph Solis, "Dream Act 2019: Dreamers, Temporary Protected Status Holders Push for Immigration Bill in Boston," Mass Live, March 18, 2019. www.masslive.com/boston/2019/03/dream-act-2019-dreamers-temporary-protected-status-holders-rally-in-boston-for-immigration-bill.html.

U.S. Citizenship and Immigration Services, "DHS DACA FAQs," uscis.gov, March 8, 2018. https://www.uscis.gov/archive/frequently-asked-questions#what_is_DACA.

Pete Williams, "DACA Protections Can Continue in 2019 after Supreme Court Doesn't Act," NBC News, January 22, 2019. nbcnews.com/politics/supreme-court/daca-protections-can-continue-2019-after-supreme-court-doesn-t-n961221.

For Further Discussion

Chapter 1

1. Will a more extensive and robust border wall solve the immigration problems the United States is experiencing? Why or why not?
2. What effect does immigrant family separation have on children? On their parents?

Chapter 2

1. Why would sanctuary cities take matters into their own hands to help immigrants? Which actions do you think are the riskiest? Why?
2. What risks are federal judges taking in opposing President Trump's immigration rules? Are these judges putting the system of government checks and balances in action?

Chapter 3

1. Do you think that learning English should be a requirement for immigrants in the United States? Why or why not?
2. How is a country's labor force affected by immigration policies?

Chapter 4

1. Is ending DACA is unconstitutional? Why or why not?
2. Did either President Obama or President Trump have the right to use executive orders to bypass Congressional approval or veto? How do their actions affect illegal immigrants?

Organizations to Contact

The editors have compiled the following list of organizations concerned with the issues debated in this book. The descriptions are derived from materials provided by the organizations. All have publications or information available for interested readers. The list was compiled on the date of publication of the present volume; the information provided here may change. Be aware that many organizations take several weeks or longer to respond to inquiries, so allow as much time as possible.

Amnesty International

1 Easton Street
London WC1X 0DW
United Kingdom
(44) 20 7413 5500
website: www.amnesty.org

Amnesty International has been helping people all over the world claim their rights since 1961. It helps refugees, asylum-seekers, and migrants get to where they need to go by pressuring governments to process necessary paperwork without bureaucratic delays.

Border Angels

P.O. Box 86598
San Diego, CA 92138
(619) 487-0249
email: info@borderangels.org
website: www.borderangels.org/

Border Angels is a nonprofit organization comprised of volunteers to fight for human rights, immigration reform, and social justice. It pays particular attention to border issues between the United States and Mexico. Border Angels also serves San Diego County's immigrants with outreach services, including legal assistance.

Center for Migration Studies

307 E. 60th Street, Fourth Floor
New York, NY 10022
(212) 337-3080
email: cms@cmsny.org
website: www.cmsny.org

The Center for Migration Studies was founded in 1964. It is affiliated with the Congregation of the Missionaries of St. Charles, a community of Catholic priests and others who are dedicated to helping migrants and refugees. The organization is a think tank and educational institute dedicated to immigrant rights and fostering greater understanding between immigrants and the communities that receive them.

Families for Freedom

35 West 31st St., #702
New York, NY 10001
(646) 290-8720
email: info@familiesforfreedom.org
website: www.familiesforfreedom.org

Families for Freedom was founded in 2002. Based in New York, it helps families who face and need to fight deportation. The organization is made up of immigrant detainees, former immigrant prisoners, and those at risk of deportation. Its goal is to repeal harmful laws and to provide a strong voice in immigrant rights.

Immigrant Defense Project

40 W. 39th St., Fifth floor
New York, NY 10018
(212) 725-6422
website: immdefense.org

The Immigrant Defense Project's mission is to ensure justice and fair treatment for immigrants in the United States. It seeks to fight against a legal system that violates basic human rights and the lives of thousands of immigrants. The organization works to shape policies and strengthen immigrant defense through training and legal advice.

International Organization for Migration (IOM)

17 Route des Morillons
1218 Grand-Saconnex
Switzerland
(41) (22) 717-9111
email: hq@iom.int
website: www.iom.int

The IOM has grown from a logistics agency to one that works with governments and civilians to foster greater understanding of migration issues, nurture social and economic development, and advocate for migrant dignity.

Migration Policy Institute

1400 16th Street, NW
Suite 300
Washington, DC 20036
(202) 266-1940
email: info@migrationpolicy.org
website: www.migrationpolicy.org

The Migration Policy Institute was founded in 2001. Its mission is to improve immigration policies through research and analysis. It develops new migration policy ideas and has become a leading institution in that field.

National Immigration Forum

50 F Street, Suite 300
Washington, DC 20001
(202) 347-0040
website: immigrationforum.org

The National Immigration Forum champions the causes and value of immigrants and immigration to the United States. Its work focuses on four areas: immigration reform and workforce needs, integration and citizenship, borders and interior enforcement, and state and local immigration developments. Overarchingly, it seeks to bridge the gap between policy and politics.

National Immigration Law Center

3450 Wilshire Blvd., #108-62
Los Angeles, CA 90010
(213) 639-3900
email: reply@nilc.org
website: www.nilc.org

The National Immigration Law Center was founded in 1979. It is one of the top organizations in America exclusively dedicated to the rights of low-income immigrants. In addition to engaging in litigation to protect the rights of these immigrants, it also analyzes policies to find solutions for immigrant health care, immigrant youth legal status, and other rights.

Office of the United Nations High Commissioner for Human Rights

Palais des Nations
CH-1211 Geneva 10
Switzerland
(41) (22) 917-9220
email: InfoDesk@ohchr.org
website: www.ohchr.org

The Office of the United Nations High Commissioner for Human Rights has a mandate to promote and protect all human rights for all people. It helps governments to fulfill their obligations. It also works to help individuals claim their rights. As part of the United Nations and its support of peace and security, human rights, and development, it speaks out against human rights violations as a nonpartisan organization.

U.S. Citizenship and Immigration Services

website: www.uscis.gov

U.S. Citizenship and Immigration Services (USCIS) is a government agency that has responsibility for lawful immigration to America. It administers the immigration system with an eye toward protecting Americans, securing the homeland, and honoring American values.

U.S. Customs and Border Protection

website: www.cbp.gov

U.S. Customs and Border Protection is a government agency with a mission to safeguard the country's borders. It is one of the world's largest law enforcement agencies and enables national trade and travel.

U.S. Immigration and Customs Enforcement

website: www.ice.gov

U.S. Immigration and Customs Enforcement (ICE) is a government agency that has responsibility to identify and conduct cross-border criminal investigations that threaten the security of the United States.

Young Center for Immigrant Children's Rights

6020 South University Avenue
Chicago, IL 60637
(773) 360-8920
email: info@theyoungcenter.org
website: www.theyoungcenter.org

The Young Center for Immigrant Children's Rights was established in 2004. It advocates for immigrant children who arrive in America on their own. The organization also works to change the immigration system in accordance with the best interests of children.

Bibliography of Books

Amanda Armenta. *Protect, Serve, and Deport: The Rise of Policing as Immigration Enforcement*. Oakland, CA: University of California Press, 2017.

Congressional Research Service. *Immigration: U.S. Asylum Policy*. Washington, DC: Congressional Research Service, 2019.

Congressional Research Service. *A Primer on U.S. Immigration Policy*. Washington, DC: Congressional Research Service, 2019.

Louis DeSipio and Rodolfo O. De La Garza. *U.S. Immigration in the Twenty-First Century: Making Americans, Remaking America*. New York, NY: Routledge, 2018.

William A. Schwab. *Dreams Derailed: Undocumented Youths in the Trump Era*. Fayetteville, AR: University of Arkansas Press, 2019.

Nikesh Shukla and Chimene Suleyman, eds. The Good Immigrant: 26 Writers Reflect on America. New York, NY: Little, Brown, 2019.

Alexis M. Silver. *Shifting Boundaries: Immigrant Youth Negotiating National, State, and Small-Town Politics*. Stanford, CA: Stanford University Press, 2018.

Matthew Soerens and Jenny Yang. *Welcoming the Stranger: Justice, Compassion & Truth in the Immigration Debate*, Revised Edition. Downers Grove, IL: Inter-Varsity Press, 2018.

Laura Wides-Muñoz. *The Making of a Dream: How a Group of Young Undocumented Immigrants Helped Change What It Means to Be American*. New York, NY: HarperCollins, 2018.

Tom K. Wong. *The Politics of Immigration: Partisanship, Demographic Change, and American National Identity*. New York, NY: Oxford University Press, 2017.

Index